Heroic (

An Optimist's Guide to Life

Philip D Groom

Groom, Philip D.
ISBN: 978-0-7443-1995-8
Heroic Quest: An Optimist's Guide to Life / Philip D. Groom –
1st ed.

SynergEbooks
948 New Hwy 7
Columbia, TN 38401
www.synergebooks.com

Cover art by Dan Saunders
Contact the author at
https://twitter.com/HeroicQuest

Printed in the USA

HEROIC QUEST

The Heroic Quest Philosophy:

Today is the most important day of your life.
Challenges & tests are unavoidable.
Happiness requires daily effort.

TABLE OF CONTENTS

Foreword
by
David Thomas GMM

David Thomas is a Guinness record breaker,
and the London Times
#1 bestselling author of 'Tell Me Why Mummy.' He is one of
the most successful people in history in his field. David
delivers motivational keynote speeches on how people
can tap into their own unlimited potential.
http://www.TheMotivationSpeaker.com

As a child growing up and through most of my twenties, I was a typical mushroom – kept in the dark and fed shit. My life was very limited. I was not encouraged to 'think outside the box' or to get ideas above my station. I struggled to deal with the simple concepts of happiness, money and success.

For these reasons and many more, I wish I had had this book.

This book is a beacon of light that would have shone through the darkness, illuminating my existence with fantastic ideas and strategies that if implemented, would have made a huge and positive difference to my life.

By reading this book, you have that opportunity awaiting you in the coming pages.

Philip has put together a book which is unique. He has that incredible skill that is given to a chosen few. The ability to write like he is talking to you over the garden fence while hitting you on the back of the head with a frying pan of a brilliant idea.

1

He writes with passion and infectious enthusiasm. Every word is infused with his total belief in what he shares.

He has the humility to know when he needs to bring in expert ideas that are not his own but then injects his down to earth humour to make it not only very readable but easy to understand.

Integrity, desire to help others and a bunch of cracking ideas that can make a massive difference. What more do you need from a book?

Prologue

What do you give the person who has everything?

The greatest gift you can give yourself, or anyone else, for that matter, is the present. If you can forget the problems of yesterday, and stop worrying about tomorrow, you won't end up ruining today. Living positively "in the now" is the only way to achieve lasting, authentic happiness.

All great endeavours start with a first step, and I believe that deciding to live in the present is the first step toward genuine happiness. The path is windy and rocky, and like most paths these days it will have its fair share of dog mess, but if you take it one step at a time, everyone can reach the end.

Somewhere in this book is the key to your happiness. It might be a particular chapter, a helpful technique, or even a simple quote, but I guarantee that there is something in here that will inspire you and put a smile on your face. Not bad for something that costs about the same as a ticket to the movies?

"Yesterday is history and tomorrow is a mystery, but today is a gift, and that is why it is called the present."

~ Alice Morse Earle

1. Today is the Most Important Day of Your Life

Three of the most significant things I have read in my life deal with the concepts of time, fear and happiness.

1. The past exists in our memories, the future in our expectations.

2. Whatever happens, I will be able to handle it.

3. Happiness requires a daily battle with your ego.

Together they make up the foundations of the **Heroic Quest Philosophy** which can be summed up in three simple statements; Today is the most important day of your life. Challenges & tests are unavoidable. Happiness requires daily effort.

Before I expand on this and give you a flavour for how these three ideas can help you on your quest for happiness, I think I had better explain how I came to find them and why I bothered to remember them.

I had a happy childhood as far as I can remember, during which I spent a lot of time with myself and my dog playing in the fields and woods near my home. I think that spending so much time close to nature with only myself to talk to, I became quite introspective and self-aware from an early age.

My mum was always doing yoga and leaving books around about meditation and history, which gave me an insight into spirituality and human nature that I found intriguing. I was particularly fascinated by the concepts of fate and destiny, and would constantly wonder how and why things happened, and how they made me feel. Dad was a bit aloof, but he was into cars and motor racing, which I also loved. He was a big strong guy with a rough exterior and a good heart, although for many years I could not see it myself. It was only after he had a triple bypass later in life that I really got to know him for who he was.

I was confident in school, but I did continually worry about what people thought about me, and made every effort to fit in and appeal to everyone. My big sister was very protective and like a second mum to me when I was little. As I grew up, you could not have wished for a better older sibling. She always looked out for me during school and when I was out and about. She let me hang out with her friends, which often involved doing things that older kids do way before the rest of my mates were (use your imagination). This helped me grow up quite quickly and gave me quite a bit of cred' because I knew a lot of the cool older teenagers where we lived.

By my early teens I had my own ideas of what I wanted from life, and the core of my hopes focused on simply being happy. When other kids wished for motorbikes or to lose their virginity, I would wish to be happy, somehow I knew that if I was happy, nothing else would really matter.

I did not talk about my thoughts with anyone else, as I assumed that everyone would also be thinking this, even though this was not always obvious from the way that most people carried on. To this day, the only wish I ever make if I see a shooting star or throw a coin into a well is the same one I made then – I want true happiness. I have been confident that, if my focus is for me to be happy in a very simple way, then everything else should fall into place.

I enjoyed school and learning, and eventually made it to college – as was expected – where I studied geology, which I loved. When I graduated, I was expecting to be an international adventurer exploring for gold or diamonds in Africa, but the reality was a career in landfill site management or working on oil rigs. I chose oil rigs, which were initially exciting and quite impressive when most of your mates worked in an office. However, the lack of space and the depressing environment of the North Sea soon took its toll, and I quit after a year. I spent the next 18 months of my life packing boxes in a warehouse, which, despite the low pay, was a fantastic and life-changing experience. I met some great people, and for the first time in years had time to think again about what I was doing and where I was going.

I then found pharmaceutical sales, which combined my fascination with people with an intellectually challenging and stimulating subject. I discovered a natural ability to summarise information quickly and effectively, communicating it with people of wide-ranging personalities and characters. I was very successful from the start and rapidly progressed to sales training and development.

This progressed into a flourishing career in sales management, which was hugely challenging, rewarding and very emotionally demanding, as you need to continually satisfy the needs of senior management, your sales team (who become like another family), your customers, and your real family, whilst maintaining a healthy balance. "All things to all men" comes to mind. I have always been comfortable with people from all walks of life, so the ability to be a bit of a human chameleon is very instinctive and natural for me. My underlying character remains the same, as do my values, so my behaviour remains congruent no matter who I'm with.

Most people assume that I am an extremely positive, optimistic person, but I am the same as everyone else and actually think my natural state is to be a bit cynical. I was hugely fortunate to have realised early on that I had a choice in how I felt, and if I made an effort to be happy, I could change my outlook in regards to any situation on any given day.

Someone once told me that if you do not like something in your life then change it, and if you cannot change it, then change your attitude to it. This obviously takes effort and often a bit of creativity. Like any useful skill, it also takes a lot of practice to get it consistently right; that is why it requires attention every day.

What is happiness?

First of all, I suppose we should really establish what happiness is.

There are many definitions, but a couple that I think work well describe happiness as:

"An optimistic, enduring state that consists of positive feelings and includes both peace of mind and active pleasures or joy."
~ Aristotle

"Happiness is a journey, not a destination; happiness is to be found along the way not at the end of the road, for then the journey is over and it's too late. The time for happiness is today not tomorrow."
~ Paul H Dunn

I think essential elements of happiness are: enjoying your life and being content with what you have and who you have with you; not wanting to be anyone else or anywhere else with anyone else; being at peace with yourself and the world around you; being comfortable in your own skin.

"Happiness is when what you think, what you say and what you do are in harmony."
~ Mahatma Gandhi

"Happiness is feeling good and wanting to continue to feel good. Unhappiness is feeling bad and not wanting to feel bad anymore."
~ Professor Richard Layard

Real happiness is not the transient pleasure associated with splurging money, getting drunk or high, or enjoying a thrill ride at an amusement park or a one night stand. It is enduring and more about serenity and contentment than gratification. Real happiness, like anything worth having, takes time to develop and nurture, and once you know what it is, it is easier to find and hold on to. Being happy doesn't mean everything is perfect; it means you have decided to look beyond the imperfections.

If you can adopt a positive attitude on a daily basis, life will be less stressful and more satisfying. You will be more useful to yourself, your family, your friends and work colleagues.

If you need further convincing or evidence, then Dr. Martin E. P. Seligman has carried out huge amounts of research backing this up, which can be found in his national bestselling book *'Learned Optimism – How to Change Your Mind and Your Life'*. Another advocate of optimism was the American polymath, Robert Anton Wilson. He researched this subject extensively and concluded that optimists are healthier, live longer and have more fun.

So come on, let's take the first step to finding the key to your authentic happiness. There's no time like the present!

Letting Go of the Past

The past exists in our memories, the future in our expectations.

Our memories are a mysterious cocktail of chemicals and electricity that nature has given us the ability to modify or erase. People are so capable of messing around with memories that they genuinely start to believe the modified truth, so much so that they can even fool a lie detector.

I know it sounds weird, but you probably do it all the time without thinking about it. I went to a music concert once and thought it was a bit average, but everyone else who saw it loved it, so in order not to spoil their enjoyment of it by telling them it was crap, I agreed and told them about the few bits I did enjoy. After a few weeks, I was recounting the gig with another friend, and I realised I was talking quite enthusiastically about it. How shallow is that? It had crept up on me without me even trying. Now I only really remember the lovely night out I had with my wife when we went to see Madonna. According to my wife, there must be some mental tinkering going on with memories otherwise most women would only ever have one child.

Some things you just can't forget, but you can try and lose your attachment to them. Letting go is a very difficult thing to do that takes a lot of effort and practice. If something is holding you back from being happy, you need to let it go whether it is a memory, a place, an object or a person. Turn your back on the thing that has power over you, and eventually its power will fade and you can choose to move on.

"One problem with gazing too frequently into the past is that we may turn around to find the future has run out on us."
~ Michael Cibenko

Expectations

Our expectations can be dealt with in several positive ways.

Either you make them simple and achievable with no attachment to their outcome, or you don't have any expectations at all and you simply live for the moment. (Not like the main character in Luke Rhinehart's 'The Dice Man' though; he lived in the moment by letting a dice decide everything for him with outrageous, illegal and immoral consequences. Please do not adopt this attitude; it is not healthy for you, or anyone else, for that matter. This is a particular favourite in Eastern philosophies, but is one that Westerners like me have a bit more trouble with due to years of brainwashing by TV and other advertising.

Advertising is incredibly powerful. It is also influential on shaping our attitudes and our expectations. Advertisers use every trick in the book to appeal to our conscious and subconscious needs and desires. According to media advertisements, in order to be happy and fulfilled, you should look like a model, drive a Ferrari, vacation in the Caribbean and live in a mansion. The more we believe and aspire to this vision of perfection, the more money we spend and the more they make.

There were companies in the 70's that used almost invisible "flash images" embedded into TV ads, each lasting less that a fraction of a second. This was known as subliminal imaging or subliminal messaging. You could be watching an ad for washing powder and a flash image of a beautiful smiling woman, wearing a brilliant white floaty dress, would be cut into the ad, so quickly that your conscious mind wouldn't see it, but your subconscious mind would. You would then associate the washing powder with happiness and sparklingly clean clothes, thus making you want to buy it over any other

11

brand. A single frame of film in the right place could influence what you thought about the product and if you bought it or not. Very clever stuff! This was eventually deemed to be a bit sneaky of advertisers and it is now illegal to use in advertising, though it is sometimes still used in TV shows and movies to create certain moods and add atmosphere, so watch out for it.

People (that includes all of us) have been conditioned toward achieving goals and aiming toward an idea of success: for example, nice clothes, expensive jewellery, a big house, a flashy car, loads of money, the perfect family, exotic holidays... the list goes on. However, chasing these expectations often leads to unhappiness because we are constantly striving for more, and not enjoying what we already have.

"The best thing about the future is that it comes only one day at a time."
~ Abraham Lincoln

"I never think of the future. It comes soon enough."
~ Albert Einstein

Choices and Simplicity

You would think that having options would allow you to select precisely what makes you happy, but too much choice often makes for misery. It seems that, as society grows wealthier and people become freer to do whatever they want, they get less happy. Having too many options can be paralysing and exhausting. It can lead us to set unreasonably high expectations, to question our choices before we even make them and blame our failures entirely on ourselves. When you have no food you are unhappy because you are hungry, but with increasing wealth and so much choice available, people now get stressed trying to decide what to have for dinner of an evening.

Don't mistake boredom for unhappiness. Lots of people get upset and frustrated when they are bored. The comedian Robin Williams said, *"Cocaine is God's way of saying that you're making too much money."* I think boredom is God's way of saying that everything in your life is fine and you haven't got anything to worry about. I think boredom is a great sign and if you make the most of it when it happens to you, you can go out and do something you enjoy while you have the luxury of time to play with. You don't stop playing because you get old; you get old because you stop playing.

Conditional happiness – i.e. happiness that is dependent on things or conditions that are outside of your control, such as winning the lottery or marrying a film star – is an endless quest. Don't let the constant desire and pursuit for material possessions determine your happiness. Don't get me wrong, we all have hopes, dreams and aspirations, but the key is not attaching too much importance to them. Don't let achieving them determine whether you are happy or not. For instance, I would love to go to the Galapagos Islands, but it is bloody expensive and out of my reach. If I one day get to go there, I will be extremely grateful and happy for a while, but if I don't ever get to visit this marvel of nature, I will not let that fact make me miserable. Great if I do; fine if I don't.

"Focus on what you have and your life will be full; focus on what you do not have and your life will be empty."
~ Unknown

With this in mind, it may be useful to have an alternative goal that focuses on what makes your soul happy. Imagine redefining your expectations and success so that they focus on things that are achievable every day, and that do not involve constantly chasing material possessions. A realistic expectation from life could be something as simple as living a full and balanced life, without harming anyone else, whilst endeavouring to be happy despite how our actions may turn out.

I think the 'past, present, future' thing is summarised quite well in the novel, 'Way of the Peaceful Warrior' by Dan Millman:

"Your sorrow, fear and anger, regret and guilt, your envy and plans and cravings live only in the past, or in the future.... 'I remember being angry in the present'... 'What you mean is you acted angry in a present moment. Action always happens in the present, because it is an expression of the body but the mind is like a phantom that lives only in the past or future. Its only power over you is to draw your attention out of the present.' A Warrior's life is not about imagined perfection. It is about love. Love is the warrior's sword. Wherever it cuts, it gives life, not death..."
~ Dan Millman

Whatever happens, I will be able to handle it

This bit focuses on the **present**; the tiny fleeting gap between what you expect (the future) and your memories (the past). It's so fleeting a period of time, it has already elapsed and is now your past. Everything you have just read is already past and is now part of your memory. Oops, there it goes again, and again... and again... and again....

So far, you have survived life, and probably been through some really scary and horrible stuff, but still, here you are. If you face the present with the attitude of "whatever happens, I can

14

handle it" because you have done so more or less successfully thus far, you won't freak out every time something you don't like or something unexpected happens.

We have all been through job interviews, confrontations with the boss, or exams, and they did not kill us, though they may have felt life-threatening at the time. Many of us have faced illness, bereavement or huge emotional events, like breaking up with someone, but we survived to tell the tale. Obviously, some things are just designed to scare the shit out of you, such as bungee jumping or skydiving. (I'm sorry, but if you're going to put yourself in these situations, you deserve to freak out a bit... but surely that's the point?)

Life can sometimes seem incredibly daunting, and trying to deal with it can feel overwhelming. It can be useful to slow down, take a step back and break it down into smaller and smaller pieces until you can cope. We have all heard the proverb "one day at a time", but when things really mount up and get on top of us, even a day can feel like forever. Sometimes the only way to deal with life is to break it down even further, until you are literally just dealing with the now.

One day at a time, one hour at a time, one minute at a time, one second at a time; step by step and inch by inch. This is the key to living in the present, and when you have done it once, you can do it again and again, even when things are going well. When you live in the present, you notice and appreciate the myriad of good things in your life that you usually take for granted.

"I need neither future nor past, but to learn to take today not too fast."
~ Jeb Dickerson

So, to tie all this past, present, future stuff up, let's see how it all looks joined together.

The past is gone, so remember the good bits and let go of the bad, because there is nothing you can do to change the past (unless your name is Marty and you have a DeLorean and a mad genius professor as your best friend).

The future exits in our expectations so make your expectations realistic, and don't let your happiness depend on whether you achieve them or not. Focus on what you have and your life will be full; focus on what you do not have and your life will be empty.

The present is the tiny fleeting gap between the past and the future, so focus on the present and appreciate the beauty and simplicity that surrounds you every day. Trust yourself and face the present with the attitude of "whatever happens, I can handle it." If anything does happen that you don't like, it will become a memory almost instantly and memories can be changed or forgotten with time.

Your mind has all sorts of safety mechanisms built into it to protect you from past physical or emotional trauma. Many people who have suffered abuse or accidents have subconsciously erased the memories from their minds, so that they can continue living their lives without having to remember the past trauma every day. This is a very complex area of psychology that I am not qualified to advise on. If this has struck a chord with you and you feel like you need to investigate some personal issues further, I highly recommend that see a qualified health care professional for advice.

Try living as happily as you can *in the now,* without trying to live up to the constant expectations of others or dwelling on the past.

I think it all seems pretty straightforward when you look at it like that, don't you agree? And hopefully this puts the first element of the Heroic Quest Philosophy into context:

Today is the most important day of your life.

Before we go rushing headlong into the next, critical part, which I will deal with in chapter 3, we need to fill in a bit of the background regarding why we feel like we do in certain situations, and why this may be important to how we react to them when they are happening. I think you're really going to find this enlightening – I certainly did when I was researching it – so sit back and discover why you and your body are both complex and amazing.

2. Even the Bravest Hero Feels Fear

"The feeling of fear (adrenalin) is as natural as the feelings of hunger and thirst. When you feel hungry, you don't panic, you eat. When you feel thirsty you don't panic, you drink. So if it is fear – you don't panic, you do."
~ Cus Damatio

Don't mistake adrenalin for fear.

Adrenalin is a funny thing. It has been the subject of whole books in itself. If you want to know more about the physiology of adrenalin and how to deal with it, there are some great books out there. One of my favourites is Geoff Thompson's *Fear: The Friend of Exceptional People – Techniques in Controlling Fear*. Geoff looks at several different ways the body releases adrenalin and how they affect your state of mind.

He also mentions that there are different types of adrenalin:

Anticipation adrenalin – slow release adrenalin that is gradually "dripped" into your body as you worry about something, like an exam or forthcoming confrontation. This slowly corrodes and wears the recipient out, leaving him feeling weak and hollow.

Pre-confrontation adrenalin – fast release "adrenal dump". This happens when a situation comes out of nowhere and you have no time to prepare. It can cause someone to freeze and panic, and is often felt as terror. This adrenalin also causes several potentially unpleasant physiological effects, such as tunnel-vision, bowel loosening (this is where the lovely phrase "I was shitting myself" comes from), the shakes, nausea, heart palpitations and dry mouth. They are all related to the body preparing for major damage as a result of the confrontation. The only way to cope with this is to stop whatever you are doing and let the terror wave sweep over you without panicking. Examine the feelings, try to relax by breathing abdominally (more on this in Chapter 3), but do not recoil or run away from the feelings.

Panic – a sudden sensation of fear that is so strong as to dominate and/or prevent reason and logical thinking, replacing it with overwhelming feelings of anxiety and frantic agitation consistent with an animalistic fight or flight reaction. This massive dump of adrenalin can easily result in panic, especially if you have never experienced it before or if it is totally unexpected, e.g. intruders in your house when you are sleeping. As we go through life, we log experiences in our brains that we refer back to time and time again. Often the reason we panic and become overwhelmed is due to the fact that we are experiencing something we have never encountered before, and we therefore have nothing to refer or anchor to and our brains go into freefall.

Imagine that your brain is a Rolodex. For the younger readers among you, a Rolodex is a rotating file device used to store business contact information. (They were very popular in the 80s.) When you face a potentially adrenalin-inducing situation, (e.g. a job interview) your brain refers to the job interview section of the Rolodex (or the next closest thing that made you nervous, such as a first date) to see how you got on last time. If it went OK, you feel fine; if it went badly, you will probably get more adrenalin, which you will have to deal with. If you come across something totally new, such as a charging elephant or being mugged, your brain can't find an index card to latch onto, so the Rolodex spins out of control, looking for a relevant card; you become overwhelmed and panic.

Fortunately, I have only had to deal with this level of intense adrenalin a few times. However, these levels do tend to happen in dangerous situations where you need to do something quickly or suffer the consequences. I have used "slap and stop" to try to bring myself back to reality. The process is known as **ASA – Accept, Stop and Act**. Literally give yourself a Slap (or somebody else might!). Stop and try to be positive, and then make a decision to do something and Act on it. Whether you fight, scream and act crazy, or run, it's important that you do something positive and deal with the situation. The only thing worse than a bad decision is no decision at all. Obviously, the best way to circumvent all this stress is by choosing to steer clear of these situations if at all possible.

"It is easier to avoid fear than to overcome it."
~ Sir Ranulph Fiennes

Pre-confrontation adrenalin, which is the most intense, can actually become quite addictive. When controlled and focused, the high that comes with it can make you feel invincible and super human. It is the reason why some people choose careers that put them in adrenalin-producing situations, such as race car driving.

Consequence adrenalin – If you fear the negative outcome of a situation or confrontation, such as reprisals, failure, or humiliation, this type of adrenalin can force you to abort whatever you are planning before you even start. This has stopped many great plans and ideas dead in their tracks. I know several people who have agreed to undertake parachute or bungee jumps who then spent weeks, even months, worrying constantly about it. This slow drip of adrenalin magnified their worries and concerns so much that on the day of the event they refused to jump or were too ill to do it.

In-confrontation adrenalin – If things are not going to plan and you need a boost, your brain can give you another kick, which again is nearly always mistaken for fear. This squirt of adrenalin, when focussed and controlled, has been attributed to many feats of super-human strength and bravery. We've all heard the stories about the old lady lifting the car off her grandchild or the soldier that was shot but did not feel it and still had the strength to save his comrades. However, if this sudden kick of adrenalin is not focussed or used, it can be totally debilitating and turn your legs to jelly in an instant.

Post-confrontation or aftermath adrenalin – After the confrontation, whether the outcome was positive or negative, you get another slow dribble of adrenalin just in case something else comes up. This is a bit like your body putting you on amber alert. This can also make you feel a bit wobbly and make you doubt yourself and your actions. A little slap and a chat (or even a bit of a cry) can really help here. Most soldiers or emergency service personnel I have met were sick after the first time they had to deal with a major situation or confrontation. It is generally accepted as part of the job and is so common that it is almost considered as a rite of passage. But once these people got used to that extra adrenalin showing up at those times, they were much better able to handle it.

Combination adrenalin – People working in highly stressful environments, such as oil rigs, the emergency services or big business, are exposed to a combination of adrenalin on a daily basis. They can experience a combination of slow drip adrenalin in anticipation of a situation, a big dump of adrenalin during unexpected or unplanned events, and aftermath adrenalin in relation to situations that have passed. This mix can be extremely "toxic" and lead to harmful levels of stress. We'll address this in more detail in Chapter 5, where we will look at the benefits of exercise in combating stress.

My personal experiences have helped me understand and deal with the effects of adrenalin and the resulting emotions. Whenever I do something new that takes me way out of my comfort zone, such as committing to a job interview, doing a charity parachute jump, or get ready to speak in public, I get an initial squirt of adrenalin that always makes me doubt myself the second I have agreed to the deed. Anyone who has agreed to be a best man at a friend's wedding will tell you that adrenalin will mess with your head from the second you agree until the moment the task is accomplished. That is why you will often hear a speech started with the classic "Being asked to be a best man is a little bit like being asked to make love to the queen; it is a tremendous honour, but you don't really want to do it."

My six year-old daughter was worried about going to school for several days, which I found unusual because she usually loves it. When I asked her why she was upset. Eventually she told me that she did not like "doing coins". When I dropped her off at school the next day, I had a quick chat with her teacher. We worked out that, up until now, she had found most lessons pretty straight forward, but she was struggling to tell how much each coin was worth and so did not know what numbers to add up. Her teacher simply said, "This is probably the first time she has come up against something in school that she does not understand straight away, and she is out of her comfort zone." Now I recognised that feeling straight away, so when Anna got home, we had a chat and she told me how she feels before "doing coins. "My tummy feels funny and I don't want to do it", she said, "I feel a bit upset and sometimes a bit sicky."

I explained to her that it is fine not to understand straight away, and that the feeling of worry she was getting was due to adrenalin. She obviously did not know what adrenalin is, so I explained that it was her brain telling her to get ready, concentrate, and try hard. "That the sicky feeling is normal, and it just means that you are getting ready to do something new."

Like little kids do, she readily accepted this parental advice, and after a few more chats she got the gist and came to understand the "adrenalin feeling" as normal. Soon after, we went to a party with loads of kids she did not know, and when we were in the car she said, "Dad, Dad I've got adrenalin again!" I reminded her that it was normal and asked her if she was OK, and she said, "Yes," and off to the party we went, where she met loads of new kids and had lots of fun. Without the reassurance that what she was feeling was normal, she may well have decided to succumb to the doubt and worry that goes with the adrenalin, and avoid the new situation in the way that kids sometimes do.

There are several reactions to adrenalin that are well recognised, "Fight or Flight" being the most commonly understood. Reactions to adrenalin can be totally crippling and overwhelming; when panic sets in they can result in Freezing or even Fainting. (Pretty handy that they all start with F.)

My personal thoughts are that the first second your mind gets a whiff of adrenalin, depending on how sensitive you are to it, your instinct, no matter how fleeting, is to totally avoid whatever it is that has caused the feeling.

Adrenalin increases your awareness of the situation, and tries to convince you to totally avoid the threat, which is pretty sensible, actually. Adrenalin tries to fill you with doubt, fear and weakness in order to make you totally reconsider doing anything but avoiding the threat. This would probably mean running away, but if the situation is particularly extreme, it could result in you freezing "like a rabbit in the headlights" or even fainting! This is not as daft as it first sounds because being on the ground gives you nowhere else to fall and therefore minimises the damage, unless of course you were on the edge of a cliff, which would be particularly unfortunate, but not entirely unheard of.

"Playing dead", whether it was up to you or adrenalin, has also saved some people from attack. I have heard about cases where bears have simply "played with" people who have fainted instead of mauling and eating them. Some people are just more sensitive to the effects of adrenaline than others. It is recognised that most extreme sports people need to do really dangerous and crazy things to get the kind of buzz that you or I would get from, say, a rollercoaster. Whether they produce less adrenalin or have more of a capacity to handle it, I don't know.

Unfortunately, running away, freezing and fainting, although being useful mechanisms for avoiding death, do not take into account future social consequences, ego, or post-adrenalin feelings and emotions. The feelings of doubt, weakness and avoidance happen to everyone, even if it is for a millisecond. The difference is how we deal with them. Feeling fear due to natural adrenalin can be crippling, and can result in anxiety and panic. If we recognise the doubts and fears we have are normal then we can face them head on and deal with them.

Animals have a single-minded natural instinct to survive. They don't spend hours worrying about what other animals will think of them if they run away from the scary bear or angry lion, they simply run away to live another day. Humans have the gift of free will, and with it, the ability to imagine every possibility. We have the freedom to choose whether to focus on the negatives or positives.

Public speaking is a great example of how our attitude can affect how we feel and react. I can spontaneously stand up in front of a group of people and talk for hours about something I am passionate about, but when I have to make formal presentations, I often become nervous and 'fearful', especially when I have had time to worry about the consequences, such as looking stupid if I mess up. This has led to sleepless nights and poor presentations in the past, but now I use all the techniques described in this book to ensure that I am single-mindedly optimistic and totally focussed on a successful presentation and a positive outcome.

Whether you expect success or failure, failing something that is important to you can be devastating. The best way to deal with loss or failure is to be in a healthy, strong frame of mind, so you may as well take an optimistic outlook and enjoy the journey, that way you will be in better condition to handle it. Imagine the best and create a positive outlook. We are all blessed with imagination and, bizarrely, your brain can't tell the difference between what has really happened and what you created in your imagination. Apparently the brain does not differentiate between the *thought* of an action and a *real* action. We will look into this further in the Chapter 4 when we investigate the uses of visualisation techniques.

Some war veterans have suggested that *"Optimism is the foundation of courage"*, as Nicholas Murray Butler says. All soldiers feel fear during battle; it is absolutely normal. The soldiers who have been labelled as brave are often the ones who made the decision to either not think about the consequences of an action at all, or they went to great lengths to only see the best outcomes for their actions, e.g. "When we go over the top, if I refuse, I will be court marshalled and shot by my own side; if I die, all this madness will be over, and if I get injured, but not killed, they will send me home to be looked after by pretty nurses."

"Pessimism has never won a battle."
~ Dwight D Eisenhower

Training (practice) is a critical element that needs to be considered. The army spend a lot of time and effort using psychological techniques to condition soldiers so that they only focus on the enemy, and are totally committed and drilled to do what they are trained for. If soldiers spent too much time thinking about consequence and potential negative outcomes, they would be constantly mentally and physically paralysed by fear. Many heroes in history were very ordinary people who, when push came to shove, got on with the job and won through. This again is often due to optimism, and because they trusted their instincts. Trusting yourself and believing that you will cope is important. As we mentioned before, you have got this far and are not dead yet, so you must have done some things right.

Two things that have inspired me in this department are Eastern teachings that suggest we all have an inner wisdom that is innate. *"Trust yourself; you know more than you think,"* by Benjamin Spock, is one of my favourite pearls of wisdom. My other favourite is, *"When the time comes, I will know what to do",* which is one of the main themes in Susan Jeffers' famous and inspiring book*, Feel the Fear and Do it Anyway.* One of my best friends is a professional singer, and he says that he still gets "nerves" before a gig. As we know, this is simply adrenalin preparing him, but he says that he has a routine to combat this and he keeps busy with setting up equipment, doing sound checks, anything, until the last minute so he does not let the adrenalin overwhelm him. He also says that when he is asked to sing without any notice at events (this happens a lot because he is very gregarious and a brilliant singer), he just does it and does not get nervous at all. He knows that when the time comes he will know what to do and therefore trusts himself to pull it off.

As we know, life unfortunately involves quite a bit of suffering. A solution and possible key to happiness is the ability to overcome suffering through focused optimism. I think that the purpose of life is to learn how to maintain optimism in the face of adversity, through constant practice and faith that it is all happening for a reason. I believe that single-minded optimism is the key to happiness. Most of us are not soldiers, but we need to train ourselves and practise being optimistic every day so that we can develop our own courage to face the challenges of daily life.

An extreme example of **irrepressible optimism** is illustrated by the author Dean Coontz, in his novel, *From the Corner of His Eyes*:

"Regardless of the severity of a setback, no matter how dreadful a blow you sustained, you can always find a bright side if you search hard enough. The key to happiness, success and mental health is to utterly ignore the negative, deny its power over you and find reason to celebrate every development in life, including the cruellest catastrophe, by discovering the bright side to even the darkest hour."
~ Dean Coontz

Mental attitude is like a lens to adrenalin. Like a kid focusing the sun's rays with a magnifying glass to burn a piece of paper, optimism can focus the effects of adrenalin and produce intense and useful energy and power. Conversely, negative thoughts and pessimism magnify its effects, rendering you scared and powerless.

Adrenalin + Optimism + Action = Courage & Strength

Adrenalin + Pessimism + Inaction = Fear & Weakness

There are levels of optimism that need to be considered with care as most things too extreme can be dangerous. Relentless optimism is very powerful and has got many people through seemingly impossible situations, but it has its time and place. There is an excellent book called *Adrift: 76 Days Lost At Sea*, which is a memoir by Steven Callahan about his survival in a life raft in the Atlantic ocean; a terrifying ordeal alone at sea in a damaged inflatable life raft. This feat of survival would definitely have required relentless optimism otherwise Steven would have just curled up and died of thirst within the first few days. However, there are types of "blind optimism" linked to survival in which nothing will stop the protagonist from trying to achieve his goal. A spawning salmon swimming upstream in flood waters will do so until utterly exhausted; a fanatical mountain climber may push himself to the absolute physical and mental limit trying to reach the summit at any cost.

Anchoring

In order to prepare for the stressful and potentially adrenalin inducing challenges, you can actually take some proactive steps to cope with them, or perhaps prevent them altogether. You may have heard of something called NLP or Neuro-Linguistic Programming. NLP is *"a therapeutic technique to detect and re-programme unconscious patterns of thought and behaviour in order to alter psychological responses."* (from 'NLP in 21 Days,' by Harry Alder and Beryl Heather).

The basic principle of NLP is that it is in an individual's power to change their own subconscious programming for the better. There are some really useful tools and techniques in NLP. One that I personally have found useful is called Anchoring. If you really want to do this justice, you should buy a decent NLP book or take a course, but to get you started, I'll take you through my interpretation of some basic concepts. (I also recommend the book *NLP in 21 Days* by Harry Alder and Beryl Heather to learn more.)

The anchor is a stimulus that triggers a specific physiological or emotional state or behaviour. There are "involuntary anchors" that are related to your past experiences, and these can illicit positive and negative responses. I like the smell of freshly cut grass and when I smell it, I feel happy and summery. I don't particularly like snakes, so when I see one I feel uncomfortable and on edge.

There are also "designer anchors", which you can deliberately create yourself to produce a desired mental state. Once you have **built an anchor,** you need to **install it** so that you can **trigger** it and use it at will. It all sounds a bit complicated I know, but we'll take it step by step and you'll soon get the gist.

To prepare yourself for a stressful situation, such as a job interview, you first need to build an anchor. Decide what positive state of mind you want to produce: confidence would be very useful in this circumstance, and recall from your memory an actual event when you felt absolutely confident. You then need to capture that state of mind so you can replicate it whenever you want to. You need to remember every vivid detail of this experience, recalling tastes, smells, feelings, sounds, images and textures, until you feel like you are actually back there in time, reliving this positive experience. Visualise it in real time and in full colour with surround sound. (There is more on visualisation later, so if you are having trouble with this bit, have a sneaky look at Chapter 6.) Remember and relive all the positive feelings associated with this memory. Then exaggerate them by 3 or 4 times so that they feel extremely vivid. This should be a very intense and pleasurable experience; if it is not, then choose a different memory or try magnifying the original one a bit more. Once you have captured this positive state of mind, you need to attach anchors to it so you can access it whenever you want.

The anchors are visual (images), auditory (sound) and kinaesthetic (physical). Keep them simple. Your visual anchor needs to be an image in your mind that you can easily recall anytime and anywhere, even in an emergency. For inducing a confident state, it might be an image of a hero of yours, or a wild animal such as a lion; anything that works for you. I personally imagine a scene very similar to the cover of this book. It reminds me of holidays and times when I have been totally relaxed and at peace.

Your Auditory anchor can be a short bit of internal dialogue, where you say something to yourself like "Be strong" or "You are great." Again, it can be anything that inspires you and makes you feel confident. The cool bit about this is that you can make the voice sound like anyone, so chose someone you particularly admire or respect so that the voice instils even more confidence. Someone like James Earl-Jones would probably be more effective than, say, Pee Wee Herman. I have a friend with an incredibly authoritative and confident inspiring quality to his voice. In all the years I have known him, I have never seen him get into a flap or lose control. I imagine he is speaking to me and it always makes calmer. Others have been instructed to imagine that their audience is in their underwear. This is not so much to make you laugh, but it's meant to make you realize that those who are listening to you are just as human as you are – the whole "we all put our pants on one leg at a time" kind of deal.

The Kinaesthetic anchor is a distinct, tactile trigger that fires the anchor's state of mind. A subtle but stimulating physical trigger brings another sense into the mix and engages an additional part of your brain, making the anchor even more effective. Some people press a knuckle on their hand, curl their toes, scratch their neck or rub their hands together. If you look for it you can see people on the TV doing it all the time when they are presenting or making speeches. Just make sure you make it discreet and simple so you can do it subtly in front of people without them knowing.

Now you need to install your anchor. This is a bit like downloading a new piece of software, so you need to do it properly the first time to make it work effectively. First you need to find a quiet place where you won't be interrupted for a good 15 minutes at least. Give yourself enough time to relax and recall your positive experience in vivid detail. Choose the state of mind you want to be able to call on, e.g. confident, brave, content, etc. Decide which physical, visual and auditory stimuli you are going to use to trigger your anchor. Recall the memory of your positive experience and exaggerate the feelings to make it stronger. Keep doing this until it becomes extremely intense and when you can really feel yourself feeling super confident, fire your physical, visual and auditory triggers at the same time so they attach themselves to the desired positive feeling.

In order to induce a feeling of calm, I imagine myself at my own personal beach. I can smell the sea and hear the waves gently lapping on the shore. I am standing in the warm water with sand under my feet and the sun on my face. I breathe slowly and deeply and try to remember how contented and tranquil I felt when I was there. I then imagine my friend with the calming voice telling me that "everything is fine" and that "whatever happens I will be able to deal with it". At this stage I will trigger my physical anchor (my secret!) and repeat the process for about 5 minutes until I fell totally relaxed and ready. I then tell myself that I am prepared to face whatever comes my way and to enjoy myself, whatever happens.

To test it, change your state of mind by briefly thinking or doing something else and then trigger your anchor again to see if it works. Repeat the process over and over adding extra detail and intensity, so that it eventually becomes super vivid –

even better than the original experience if you can. If you do this enough times, it will be impossible for you to trigger your anchor and not induce the desired state of mind. It is a type of self-hypnosis, so it's up to you how much you practice and how vivid you make it.

Check the anchor again the next day to confirm it is permanent. Then use it in a real life situation as soon as you can. Practice using it in "low grade" situations – don't wait for that big occasion for your first try. Also try triggering your anchor when you are feeling really confident or when you feel especially positive; this will strengthen and reaffirm your anchor state of mind. I also recommend that you fire your anchor every few weeks even if you don't need it, in order to future proof yourself for when you do.

Any time you are feeling particularly happy or pleased with yourself for achieving something, activate your anchors so that you associate them with good feelings and add to their effectiveness.

I once received two pieces of advice from an ex-manager of mine. They were "When you develop momentum, keep it going" and "Celebrate your successes." Keep these in mind when developing your anchors.

I know several professional performers and speakers who have used anchors for years, and they still trigger their anchors before big events, even if they are feeling fine. The expert who taught me still does even though he is super confident and probably does not need to anymore. Next time you watch a politician speaking on TV, watch their hands to see if you can spot them triggering their physical anchors, especially if they are feeling threatened. I've developed several anchors over the years, all with different triggers for different circumstances. I find them very comforting and reassuring. They cost nothing and don't weigh anything so they are easy to carry around: I don't leave home without them!

Try to embrace the uncertainty of new situations, and remember that even the bravest of heroes have experienced fear. In every hero there is a seed of doubt and in every coward there is a spark of courage. You actually can't have courage without fear. Courage is the act of reacting in spite of your fear(s).

Hopefully you get the gist of why you have been feeling like you have all your life and you now have some tool that will help you handle these feelings.

3. Challenges and Tests are Unavoidable

"A hero is an ordinary individual who finds the strength to persevere and endure, in spite of overwhelming obstacles."
~ Christopher Reeve, Superman (1952-2004)

Whether you like it or not, life is a never-ending series of heroic quests

An interesting and clever chap called Joseph John Campbell noticed that all myths and legends follow a similar pattern. He travelled the world investigating stories and folklore and wrote a book entitled *The Hero with a Thousand Faces*. In the book it says that basically all myths follow a basic cyclical formula, comprising of tests and trials that have to be passed in order for one to win the ultimate prize. Similarly, in our everyday lives, when faced with challenges, we also follow a cycle of feelings and actions until the quest is complete (Figure 1).

First off, we are called to action in order to sort out a problem that has cropped up in our life. We initially refuse to accept the challenge because generally we don't like change and try to avoid it. Then we face a load of unavoidable issues and complexities that force us to cross "the threshold" and accept the adventure. Then the quest really heats up. On the way, we face tests and trials in which we are assisted by friends and helpers. This goes on for a bit, but we stay the course because it is character building and we are committed. Eventually we overcome the obstacles, usually with a really meaty "ultimate challenge" and finally return home with the prize to a hero's welcome; brilliant! Then it all starts all over again because that's what life does, whether we like it or not.

I was first introduced to the Heroic Quest cycle at a business seminar, where it was used to illustrate the series of events that are faced by sales people every day. The basic gist in the commercial world is that challenges occur that prevent sales. They tend to be difficult to overcome, so they are avoided, until the boss tells you to sort them out. You realise that targets may not be achieved and that you may lose your job, so you try to find solutions. This requires help from colleagues and customer advocates. A comprehensive, SMART (more on this in chapter 6) business plan is executed and the deal is closed. This is then celebrated and rewarded with financial bonuses so that you remember to do it again next time.

I immediately recognised that this pattern of events was happening to me every day in my personal life and that I was facing loads of quests, big and small, every day. I decided from then on that when faced with challenges I would try to remember that it was completely normal – that it has been happening to people for thousands of years – and that if I followed the quest cycle to its natural end, I would eventually win through.

Figure 1. The Heroic Quest cycle, by Joseph Campbell (1904-1987)

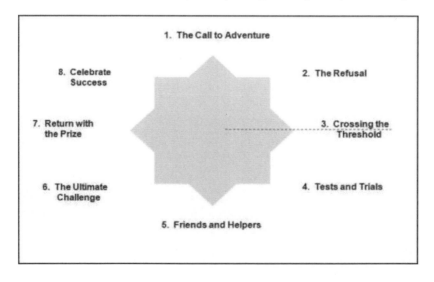

1. The Call to Adventure

8. Celebrate Success

2. The Refusal

7. Return with the Prize

3. Crossing the Threshold

6. The Ultimate Challenge

4. Tests and Trials

5. Friends and Helpers

Life imitates art and vice versa! Nearly every decent adventure film you have seen follows this cycle.

In *Star Wars*, Luke Skywalker gets the "call" from Obi-Wan and Princess Leah. Luke initially refuses (due to obligations he promised to fulfil at home), but the bad guys ransack his home and kill his family, so he has to do something. He bumps into a 7-foot hairy Wookie and a space pirate in a bar who help him battle the dark side and the Storm Troopers. Luke narrowly escapes death a few times, has a space dogfight with Darth Vadar (the villain who also happens to be his dad), blows up the death star, and finally returns with his mates to a hero's welcome. Big party and celebration – everybody's happy!

The Lord of the Rings trilogy is also a classic example of this cycle being used effectively. Hobbit gets call from wizard; Hobbit refuses; but evil threatens his homeland and he's forced to start the scary journey with other Hobbits, lots of adventures; you know the drill.

Now I'm not saying that we get asked to save the world on a daily basis; however, life is full of challenges and quests for each of us. Illness, career change, divorce, bereavement, moving, changing schools, interviews, sporting events, public speaking… the list is endless. Here's an interesting statistic: fear of public speaking is reported to be the number one fear of American adults. According to studies, public speaking is a bigger fear than death.

The point is, life is a series of challenges that, as human beings, we have been tackling since we first crawled out of the primeval ooze. These quests can last 5 minutes (having a bump in your car in busy traffic), 5 hours (a job interview), 5 days (applying for a mortgage), 5 months (dealing with a relationship issue) or 5 years (a battle with a disease); the time period is variable depending on the nature and magnitude of the quest.

There is a fantastic book that illustrates beautifully the heroic quest, called *Eat, Pray, Love* by Elizabeth Gilbert. It is the true story of Elizabeth Gilbert (played by Julia Roberts) looking for her 'meaning of life'; who is she and why is she here, etc. After suffering a divorce, Liz decides to do something for herself. She jets off to Rome where she **eats** delicious food and meets some nice people who teach her to 'live' and speak Italian. Next, she travels to Delhi and joins an ashram where she learns to forgive herself through **prayer** and meditation. She makes more friends along the way who admire her, and she changes their lives by helping them learn to love and forgive. She ends her year-long quest in Bali, where she is guided by a medicine man named Ketut. She finally lets go of her past and finds her balance in life while learning to **love** again.

Elizabeth summarises her experience with a great paragraph that she calls the "Physics of the Quest":

"If you are brave enough to leave behind everything familiar and comforting, and set out on a truth-seeking journey (either externally or internally), and if you are willing to regard everything that happens to you on that journey as a clue, and if you accept everyone you meet along the way as a teacher, and if you are prepared – most of all – to face and forgive some very difficult realities about yourself... then truth will not be withheld from you."

Accept the challenge and battle through the cycle until you get the prize. Challenges are part of life, they are unavoidable and they follow a pattern, so try to embrace them and tackle them with positive thinking, optimism and self-belief, because the alternative is miserable. If you can face life's quests with a smile on your face, you are on the path to happiness.

Aristotle (384 BC – 322 BC; Greek philosopher, student of Plato and teacher of Alexander The Great) is widely accepted as being a pretty clever and wise bloke, and he told us all the answer years ago, so don't take my word for it:

"Happiness is the meaning and the purpose of life, the whole aim and end of human existence."
~ Aristotle

So there you have it. The second element of the Heroic Quest Philosophy: Challenges and tests are unavoidable.

Now at first this may seem a bit heavy and too much hard work, but the other half of the quest rewards all this effort with prizes, friends and helpers and celebration. Life is a balance of good and bad, light and dark, peaks and troughs and without lows you would not appreciate the highs.

What is the meaning of life, the Universe and Everything? For all fans of Douglas Adams's fantastic book *The Hitchhikers Guide to the Galaxy*, the answer to this question will already be known to you as 42, and if you're happy with this then you are either very eccentric or incredibly enlightened. I'll let you decide. For the rest of us a bit more pondering may be required.

Obviously, this is a question that has kept theologians and philosophers busy for millennia, and I must admit I have pondered over it few times myself. Now I am not claiming to have found the answer, and even if I really had, it would probably cause a war or something, so this is just my way of comprehending life and why we are here.

I have tried to summarise the best bits I've read or heard over the years to come up with a simple answer to the question, "What is the meaning of life?"

You could spend your whole life chasing the answer to this question, so when I read the next sentence, it was a huge relief. It made me think maybe I should stop bothering to try to understand life and simply just get on with living it:

Life is a mystery that the human mind is not capable of comprehending; some mysteries are simply not supposed to be understood.
~ Marlo Morgan – *Mutant Message Down Under*

A good friend of mine argues the case (quite regularly, in fact) that everything is natural, so everything that is happening is also natural, such as pollution and global warming. Most people try to counter this with, "Cars aren't natural and neither are spaceships, nuclear bombs or cans of diet coke." However, we are part of nature and we created all this stuff, so by default it is also nature and part of the natural order of things. If this is not the case, then where do oil, birds' nests and the barrier reef fit into it all?

We all know life can be really shit at times, such as when someone you love dies, you get ill or get your heart broken, but this stuff is happening to everyone all the time and there is simply no avoiding it. We spend a lot of time and energy trying to control things and maintain the status quo; for some reason most of us are terrified of change and do our utmost to avoid it. One of the only constants in life is that things change. You are born, you live, you age and you die. There is absolutely, positively no way to avoid it, so the moment you accept it and go with the flow, paradoxically, the more in control you will feel. Change is not merely necessary in life, it *is* life.

    o   *Trust that everything is happening perfectly as part of a grand design; pain and suffering is unavoidable and optimism is the antidote.*

You need a bit of purpose in life; otherwise why would you get out of bed in the morning? The following pearl of wisdom also explains why life is a gift, and if you use it wisely, you can be happy now.

    o   *Life may have no real purpose other than to become a better person day by day. It is an opportunity to discover what makes you happy and what your gifts or talents might be; to learn how to be at peace and content with who you are.*

Pretty obvious really. I think the old philosophers and theologians have been milking it a bit, overcomplicating things in order to look clever and to keep themselves in jobs.

Perfect Moments

"There are no perfect people or perfect lives – only perfect moments." Unconfirmed (I'll explain in a minute.)

You won't believe where I found this one. I was reading an article about Sylvester Stallone who played Rocky in the series of boxing films of the same name. He also wrote and directed the first *Rocky* film, which many people either do not know or have forgotten. He has spoken frankly about his life and how he was not particularly happy or at peace for long periods during his illustrious "A" list career, despite all the money and adoration he received. As well as being an actor, writer, and director, he is also an accomplished artist, which he says gives him moments of perfection and satisfaction. Mr Stallone can't be sure whether he read the "perfect moments" quote or invented it, but I think it is a great observation, and really puts life into perspective. Life is a mysterious tapestry interwoven with infinite moments of perfection; we just need to develop the clarity and patience to recognise them. This requires focus, discipline and practise.

Moments of perfection can take many forms: a flower; a snowflake; a child's laughter; a smile from someone you love; a cold beer on a hot day; the sun on your skin; a piece of music; the first bite of a piece of hot buttered toast; a thunderstorm... the list is endless. They are everywhere if you choose to find them. And they are often the simple things that most people take for granted. Perfection can be joy, peace, happiness, calm, clarity, love, balance, optimism, euphoria, serenity or even enlightenment.

It would seem to me that the reason that highly spiritual people find enlightenment is that they practise every day, and consistently and naturally recognise the moments of perfection so that they add up to form continuous perfection.

We spend most of our time and energy striving for control and perfection, trying to create or hold on to the perfect life or to be a perfect person, we are so preoccupied with the past and the future that we miss the perfection in the present, the magic of the everyday!

Eastern spiritual and religious traditions also recognise the concept of living in the present and appreciating the moment; they call it "mindfulness." Mindfulness is about being completely in touch with, and aware of, the present moment, as well as taking a non-evaluative and non-judgmental approach to your inner experience and thoughts. This is often achieved during meditation, where you let go of your thoughts and let them float freely through your mind by attaching no meaning or importance to them. "Less is more" is a phrase that is used in all areas of life, but it fits in here nicely. The more you let go of striving for the perfect life, the more time you create to enjoy the moments of perfection that surround you. These moments, where you are able to appreciate the beauty, perfection and simplicity of everyday life, eventually multiply and join together to produce many moments. The more you let go, the more you get back.

We will have a proper look at meditation in a minute, so relax and get ready for the next step toward a calmer and happier you.

Start Slow and Let it Grow

The thought of becoming a super optimistic person with a never-ending supply of positivity is a bit daunting for most people, myself included. It can feel like a huge challenge (which of course it is!) that you may not want to take on. Being a bit miserable is not so bad, is it? As with all things, the secret is finding a balance. Work hard at being optimistic and trust that it will bring fulfilment more than negativity, pessimism and doubt.

The best way to tackle this is one day at a time, one step at a time. If that is too much to start, try one *hour* at a time; and if that is too much, try one *minute* at a time. And if that is still too much, try one *second* at a time. If you get a handle on that, then you have tasted living in the moment, which is what most Eastern philosophies see as being the way to go toward pure bliss or happiness.

The following is a quote from *Shogun* by James Clavell. It is the advice from a teacher to a geisha:

"Always remember child that to think bad thoughts is really the easiest thing in the world. If you leave your mind to itself it will spiral you down to ever increasing unhappiness. To think good thoughts, however, requires effort. This is one of the things that discipline and training is about. So strain your mind to dwell on sweet perfumes, the touch of these silk, tender raindrops against the shoji, the curve of this flower arrangement, the tranquillity of dawn. Then at length you won't have to make such a great effort, and you will be of value to yourself and to our profession - and bring honour to our world....."

Now let's hold on to that idea for a minute while we have a look at the next bit.

Happiness Requires a Daily Battle with your Ego

I think it is extremely healthy to work towards self-awareness and personal growth as long as you do not become egotistical and obsessed with yourself.

"Knowing oneself" is critical to self-development as long as you remember not to become fixated with you! No man (or woman) is an island.

A Calm Mind Welcomes Wisdom

"Our minds are not like clear water in a crystal glass; rather, they are like water in a pond. If the water in the pond is not stirred, it will naturally settle and become clearer and clearer. However, if you feel a need to clean the pond and remove it of all things that might make it muddy and cloudy, you will only stir all the muck that had settled to the bottom. Do not be so curious as to what lay hidden in the mud. You may start pulling

on something at the bottom that you feel is garbage and end up pulling a lot of silt with it. The water was already quite clean until you started to move things around. We do the same thing with our minds. We are constantly thinking about, watching or repressing our wandering thoughts. If you start chasing away every thought that arises in your mind, or search for the intention that caused such a thought to arise, then you will never become clear. Examining yourself in this way only serves to make you more confused."
~ Buddhist Master, Sheng-yen

Before we go any further, I must add a little caveat to this. Psychotherapy and psychoanalysis are incredibly powerful and useful, and have helped countless people. If you are having mental health problems or have suffered trauma in your past, a good mental health physician will certainly be able to help. It's probably best to speak to your family doctor first as they will know who the good ones are and will help find the right one for you.

Meditation: Another Free Gift you can Give Yourself

Attention! This is not just for monks and hippies. Many top leaders, athletes and captains of industry use meditation and breathing techniques to combat stress and make them more effective.

"The gift of learning to meditate is the greatest gift you can give yourself in this life. For it is only through meditation that you can undertake the journey to discovering your true nature, and so find the stability and confidence you will need to live, and die, well. Meditation is the road to enlightenment."
~ *The Tibetan Book of Living and Dying,* by Sogyal Rinpoche

Through meditation practice, it's possible to develop a positive and clear state of mind. During meditation, you gently let go of the external distractions so you can genuinely be calm, clear, and in the present. This state of being in the present is actually a very natural one. Animals, for one, live their whole lives in the present. Although being aware of the moment is so simple, you may have spent years covering it up with all sorts of distractions, so you have to practise in order to reconnect with this concept. That's why meditation is so important.

There are literally hundreds of different methods and techniques for meditating, and finding a place to start can often be off-putting. I have provided a nice simple one to start with. For some people this will be all they will ever need, but if you want to try something different get a book, take a training course, and give it a go.

Here is a simple breathing meditation technique: First, find a calm tranquil place where you can guarantee you won't be disturbed for at least 20 minutes. Sit down in a comfortable posture. Your back should be straight, neither too stiff nor too loose. Your posture should not make you feel sleepy, and neither should it make you feel uncomfortable.

If closing your eyes helps you achieve a better focus, do so. Otherwise, just look straight ahead without actually looking at anything specific. Finding a room that has little distractions for you, as well as soothing colors and/or lighting is helpful as well.

Now put your attention on your breath. Breathe in through your nostrils and out through your mouth. If you keep your tongue pressed gently on your upper palate when you breathe in it works even better for some reason.

People tend to breathe in a slightly abnormal way; they tend to hold in their stomachs, make little use of their diaphragm, and breathe using the muscles of their upper chest, neck and shoulders. This is not the most effective way to get the needed oxygen to our brain and muscles. If you watch babies or animals breathe, you will notice that they breathe with their whole bodies, their bellies rise and fall with each breath. This is commonly known as abdominal breathing, and for some reason, we stop doing this as we grow into adulthood. My seven-year-old daughter still does it, but older kids I know don't, and I have to consciously make the effort otherwise I revert to uptight, grown-up breathing.

Abdominal breathing is the single most effective strategy for stress reduction. A person's normal breathing rate is about 8-12 breaths per minute. When someone is stressed or having a panic attack, they tend to breathe faster and more shallowly. Although they may seem to be breathing more, they are not actually getting as much oxygen in and their breathing is not as effective as it could be.

Abdominal breathing means breathing fully from your abdomen or from the bottom of your lungs. It is exactly the reverse of the way you breathe when you're anxious or tense, which is typically shallow and high in your chest. If you're breathing from your abdomen, you can place your hand on your abdomen and see it rise each time you inhale. You'll find that abdominal breathing will help you relax any time you are feeling anxious.

To practice abdominal breathing, follow these steps:

1. Place one hand on your abdomen right beneath your rib cage.

2. Inhale slowly and deeply through your nose into the bottom of your lungs. Your chest should move only slightly while your stomach rises, pushing your hand up.

3. When you've inhaled fully, pause for a moment and then exhale fully through your mouth. Purse your lips and imagine that you are blowing on a hot spoonful of soup. As you exhale, just let yourself go and imagine your entire body going loose and limp. It should take you twice as long to exhale as it did to inhale.

4. In order to fully relax, take and release ten abdominal breaths. Try to keep your breathing smooth and regular throughout, without gulping in a big breath or exhaling suddenly.

The rhythm of your breath may change as you start focusing on it. Sometimes it may get heavier, and sometimes lighter and faster. Don't worry about the change. Just keep your attention focused on your breath. Be with your breath as you inhale and exhale. The object of meditation is the sensation of breathing.

As you go deeper into the meditative state, you will automatically feel other thoughts leaving your mind. At first you may feel a sudden rush of thoughts trying to get your attention. Don't let it bother you. Don't fight your thoughts either. If you resist your thoughts, they will usually lead you astray. Just accept them, acknowledge them and as you see your attention wandering, bring it back gently to your breath again.

After some practice the "mental chatter" will stop and the distracting thoughts will leave you alone as they won't find any host willing to give them a place to linger in.

Think of any distracting thoughts as fine, floating dust in the air. In our normal state of awareness, the dust is there, but we don't notice it because we are too busy getting on with our lives. Once you still your mind, it's like the sudden calming of the wind. As the wind dies down and you become more aware of the dust, you tend to notice it more. Just remember that it was always there. The dust will settle down by itself as there is no wind to carry it around anymore. Just be patient and as they say, let the dust settle.

In the beginning you can keep an alarm clock with you, set to 15 minutes, and you can come out of your meditation when it rings. With practice you will actually be able to instruct your mind to come out of meditation after a desired span of time. If you find it impossible to sit still for 15 minutes, start with 5 minutes. Sometimes it helps to listen to soft instrumental music while you meditate. And it's best to try to mediate at the same time every day if at all possible, though that's not a hard and fast rule. Everyone is different. And if you don't get it right away, that's okay. Just keep trying. Don't give up. Even sitting in silence helps to reduce your stress.

Now how was that?

The more you practise meditation the easier and more natural it will feel. Try meditating at least once a day, starting in the morning so you are set up for the day. If it works for you, try a few more techniques, there are literally hundreds of variations so have a dig around and find one you get on with best.

So there it is. I'll quit while I'm ahead and leave it at that. Now you understand the meaning of life, or at least how to make your life happier and more fulfilling, this should free up a bit of spare time for you so you can concentrate on living life as happily as you possibly can be right now.

Depending on who you are, and what you have been through, you may be at different stages of the heroic quest cycle. In order to proceed with your journey, you may need to address some issues and get rid of some baggage.

Don't let your past hold you back. It's now your time to let go and release the hero that has always been inside you but has just needed a bit of help and encouragement to break free.

4. Let Go and Release Your Inner Hero

Eastern philosophies generally suggest that all sentient beings strive to avoid suffering and achieve happiness, and that for you to be happy you should help as much possible to assist in achieving this goal; shift focus from oneself to others, starting with family and close friends and eventually considering the needs of all sentient beings. We all too often think that when someone does us an injustice, we will only be able to forgive them when they have learnt their lesson by suffering as we have. Actually we end up focusing on ourselves and using our energies to "punish" them so that we feel that justice has been done. This always ends up with nobody feeling any happier. The great sage Homer Simpson can be quoted as saying, *"Hatred is a cage; set yourself free!"*

Generally, forgiveness is a decision to let go of resentment and thoughts of revenge. The act that hurt or offended you may always remain a part of your life, but forgiveness can lessen its grip on you and help you focus on other, positive parts of your life so you can move on. Forgiveness can even lead to feelings of understanding, empathy and compassion for the one who hurt you. Forgiveness doesn't mean that you deny the other person's responsibility for hurting you, and it doesn't minimize or justify the wrong. You can forgive the person without excusing the act. Forgiveness brings a kind of peace that helps you to go on with life.

There is a great piece on forgiveness in William P. Young's book *The Shack*. It goes something like this:

"Forgiveness is not about forgetting. It is about letting go of another person's throat. Forgiveness is first for you, the forgiver. To release you from something that will eat you alive; that will destroy your joy and your ability to love fully and

51

openly. Forgiveness in no way requires you to trust the one you forgive." "....anger is the right response to something that is wrong, but don't let the anger and pain and loss you feel prevent you from forgiving him and removing your hands from around his neck. You may have to declare your forgiveness a hundred times the first day and the second day, but the third day will be less and each day after, until you will realise that you have forgiven completely."

I think the gist is that revenge and hate are so destructive and toxic that no matter how counter-intuitive it feels, forgiveness is the only option if you want to retain any semblance of real happiness.

"Darkness cannot drive out darkness; only light can do that. Hate cannot drive out hate; only love can do that."
~ Martin Luther King Jr.

"Before you begin on the journey of revenge, dig two graves!"
~ Proverb

Karma

It is probably worth having a quick look at Karma, as it relates to our actions and how they affect us and the people around us. This is a word – and concept – that has been bandied around a lot, but not necessarily understood.

Karma is an Indian word that is part of Buddhist philosophy. It refers to a person's fate in his or her life; a fate carved in stone because of deeds done in a previous life. Good deeds give a better position in this life, while bad deeds do the reverse, just as the deeds of this life would completely affect the next rebirth. A person is reborn into the world time and again until, after enduring, suffering and learning through many lifetimes,

52

she/he becomes perfect at long last, going to nirvana, the place of perfect peace, never having to suffer rebirth again.

The philosophy of karma is that, in every moment, you are the result of your karma. It is not something that comes to you later on, or haunts you; it is each moment and only that moment. For any single action to take place, a multitude of other actions/events must have lined up to allow that event to be.

Common examples of bad karma that will 'catch up' with a person are negative things a person does, such as stealing, cheating, lying, etc. Each of these very actions, when they are being committed, is a punishment in itself. Each of these actions is like withholding water from a flower. The flower gets weaker and duller; slowly it shrivels up and dies as a result of the actions.

Common examples of good karma that will 'catch up' with a person are positive actions, such as helping others, donating money or time to a good cause, etc. Each of these actions, when they are being committed, is the actual reward. The joy that is received from helping others in a tough situation or giving out love and compassion is like a flower receiving fertilizer; the flower grows that much stronger and brighter.

Reframing – Considering Another Person's Frame of Mind

If you cast your mind back to Chapter 2, we had a quick look at the concept of NLP (Neuro Linguistic Programming). NLP deals with ideas and skills that help us to understand other people's points of view. One of these concepts is referred to as 'reframing'. Basically, reframing considers that your frame of mind in any given situation may be very different to the person or people standing right next to you. What you see is not necessarily what other people see, and vice versa. This can result in very different, and often unexpected, reactions and behaviours to things that are happening around you. It's about trying to put yourself 'in the other person's shoes', as they say. You could be in your car on a beautiful sunny day, driving through the stunning countryside, listening to great music, smiling your head off, and the person coming toward you may have a face like thunder. "Why are the sour-faced buggers not also smiling on such a beautiful day? Some people are just so ungrateful and miserable," you might think. But perhaps they have just received some devastating news or that they are driving to a funeral. The point is, the situation may appear the same, but their frame of mind can be very different to yours. Therefore, their reactions, expressions and body language will be very different.

My father-in-law is a very good driver, and in his mind everyone else is a *bad* driver. Every time anyone overtakes him, pulls away from a junction, or does anything "wrong" in a car, he has to criticise their lack of skill and judgement. He never seems to consider the other driver's point of view. This causes him no end of stress and frustration because he just can't understand why everyone else is so incompetent. The person who has just overtaken him could be rushing his pregnant wife to hospital, for heaven's sake! This results in even short journeys being quite stressful and not enjoyable for him and his passengers.

My wife, on the other hand, does understand, and always seems to subconsciously consider the other road user's point of view. I actually learnt reframing from her, way before I went on an NLP course, and it is her considerate nature that helped me understand the concept. Car journeys with her are very relaxed and I nearly always fall asleep.

In essence, try not to let other people's attitudes and reactions negatively affect yours, because you do not always know what is happening in their lives. If you are having a good day, don't expect everyone else to be having one too. Try not to impose your expectations and standards on other people.

Share your smile, but don't be too disappointed if it is not returned straight away; it will come back to you eventually. Conversely, if you are having a bad day, be mindful of what you are projecting and consider how people may be reacting to you.

"My actions are my only true belongings. I cannot escape the consequences of my actions. My actions are the ground upon which I stand."
~ Thich Nhat Hanh

"Everything happens for a reason" is a phrase that is commonly used during times of strife. Sometimes, events and situations that look and feel bad at the time often turn out for the best with the passing of time. Hindsight and all that! A few years ago, I put an offer in on a house that my wife and I had our hearts set on. We thought it was perfect and were desperate to buy it. At the very last minute in negotiations the estate agent contacted us to tell us that the owners had accepted a higher offer and we had lost the house. We had been "gazumped" (Gazumping occurs when a seller accepts a verbal offer of the asking price from one buyer, but then accepts a higher offer from someone else.) and were angry and felt totally cheated; it was all so unfair. Many older, wiser people around us said not to worry, and that something better would come along. We could not see it at the time, but then a few weeks later something better came along. Firstly my wife became pregnant, and secondly we found a beautiful house in the country, which would be perfect for bringing up a family. Karma?

Some things are a total pain in the butt, with absolutely no apparent benefit either in the short- or long-term. These bumps in the road are sent to help us develop our patience and our ability to 'let go'. Patience is the capacity to accept or tolerate troubling or suffering without getting angry or upset. The Japanese say that patience is holding back your inclination to the seven emotions: hate, adoration, joy, anxiety, anger, grief and fear, and that if you don't give way to these emotions, you will be on the path of tranquillity and in harmony with eternity. I like the way that sounds. Of course, not succumbing to all these emotions is a bit of a task, especially for the Italians among us, and requires practice and discipline. The only things that we can truly control are our reactions to whatever life hands us, so it is probably worth trying to develop this discipline if you are to stand any chance of being happy.

Some situations are simply there to test and develop our ability to let go. The ability to let go of your attachment to things, emotions and events is fundamental to achieving harmony, tranquillity, serenity... or more simply put... happiness. If you can let go of your attachments, you have really done it in the quest for happiness. Nothing will really be able to push your buttons and make you feel really unhappy again. Of course, we don't want to turn into unfeeling stones, it is absolutely fine and natural to feel any emotions as long as you don't anchor yourself to them and become obsessed with your reactions to them.

Little things can set you off. I had a Swiss army knife that I had bought with my own money when I was a kid. That knife went on every holiday and adventure with me for nearly 20 years and was still sharp. One day, I lost it, and because I had attached so much to it, I was upset for weeks. Every time I thought about it, I would obsess about where it was and how stupid I was to have lost it. I really beat myself up over this and was grumpy for ages. How could something so simple have affected me so much? Eventually, I got another knife, which of course was never quite as good as the original, and over the years I have let go of the old one emotionally. If I had just let go from the start, I would have suffered far less. The knife certainly did not care or benefit from the fact that I mourned it so much. I would have been far better off with the old *"c'est la vie"* attitude and saved myself a lot of unnecessary turmoil for nothing.

Bigger things, like the end of a relationship or loss of a loved one, are much more complex to deal with. However, experience shows us that, with time, even these things can be recovered from. I am not saying that it is easy to let go, but it is a start and can give you something to focus on when everything feels like it is spinning out of control. Apparently, enlightened Zen masters are able to deal with anything because they have developed the ultimate control in not attaching to anything. Instead of thinking of something as yours or worrying about losing it, practice being grateful for the time you have with that person, place or thing. (Another example of living in the "now.")

Now don't start worrying about the fact that you find it difficult to let go. It takes time, effort and daily, if not hourly focus, to start to flow in harmony with the world. I find that when I succumb to self-preoccupation, my whole world focuses on me and the negatives in my life. I decide that I will hold back from being happy until I get something I have decided will this time surely make me happy. "I will be happy when I get that job, meet my true love, finish that project, buy a bigger house, get a giant TV, move to the country, and lose weight." The list could run and run...why not be happy now?

I do know that I really feel good when I don't think about myself too much, instead thinking about the needs of others. Simple things, like cutting my mother-in-law's hedge or getting my wife flowers when I haven't even done anything wrong, always make me feel good. I think the Buddhists call it being 'wisely selfish'; I like that. You do something nice knowing that it will make you feel good, so you do it every now and again simply for that reason. It's definitely a bit selfish, but no harm done and a bit of happiness given in exchange. Yes, I am definitely a fan of being 'wisely selfish', and shall not feel guilty about it ever again.

"Great opportunities to help others seldom come, but small ones surround us daily."
~ Sally Koch

Worry is a Wasted Emotion

Worrying about what other people think about you is an all too common route to unhappiness. In my experience, most people are too busy worrying about themselves to really give a stuff about you, so try to forget that source of unhappiness straight away. As you mature, this one becomes clearer with every passing day. Try to adopt the attitude of older people and don't waste what little time you have left on this planet worrying about other people, who are probably more miserable than you anyway.

Here are a few titbits to contemplate:

- 95% of all things we fear never actually happens, so 95% of the time we are worrying for nothing.

- Worrying is praying for what you don't want.

- Worry is like paying interest on a debt you may never incur.

58

"In this life here are only two things to worry about. Either you are well or sick.

If you are well then there's nothing to worry about. If you are sick, there are still only two things to worry about; you get well or you die.

If you get well, there's nothing to worry about. If you die there are still only two things to worry about. Either you go to heaven or you go to hell.

If you go to Heaven, there's nothing to worry about, and if you go to hell you'll be so busy meeting all your old friends you won't have time to worry."
~ Unknown

My favourite bit of advice comes from Dr. Daniel Amen's 18, 40, 60 Rule:

"At 18 you worry about what everyone thinks of you.
At 40 you don't care.
At 60 you realise no one was thinking about you anyway!"

If only someone had sat me down when I was younger and gone through this one with me; I might have got a bit more out of being a teenager instead of worrying what colour my hair should be! Youth is wasted on the young and all that....

Wanting What you Already Have

This is a great lesson to learn and one that, when I get to grips with it, makes me feel a million dollars. Oops! There I go again 'cos I don't have a million dollars and would probably not be any happier if I did. Or would I?

59

Nine out of ten millionaires surveyed were still miserable despite their financial status.

My favourite millionaire saying is, "The two best days of owning a luxury yacht are the day you buy it and the day you sell it." The expectation is exciting, but when you actually get the yacht, you realise that it is such an exhaustingly expensive luxury that you won't be happy again until you get rid of it, and you have been so focussed on trying to get more money that you never managed to use the damn thing anyway. See, even the ultimate object of desire does not deliver guaranteed happiness. Another TV myth busted!

It appears that very rich people only start cheering up when they get bored of all the things that were distracting them from pursuing genuine happiness and they decide to give their money to people who really need it. Ironic, isn't it? Go on, find a happy millionaire and you will probably find that he/she is either mad or is secretly helping people. Some people think that you are only a real millionaire when you have *given away* a million. A friend of mine, on reading this, said, "The nicest people I have met in 22 years in banking are the ones living with their heads just above water and the worst are those who have too much money."

"Love and work, work and love ... that's all there is."
~ Sigmund Freud

Freud suggested that love and work are the cornerstones of our humanness. It appears, that work, whether it is paid or voluntary, is essential, and that we all need to love if we are to fully appreciate and enjoy life. As human beings we generate a lot of love, and it needs an outlet. Often, the more we love, the happier we are. As long as you are letting it flow, you can love your partner, your kids, your friends, a pet or even a plant, but you do need an outlet or else a bit of you dies inside.

Professor Richard Layard's book, *Happiness – Lessons from a New* Science, is one of several that reflect on the research undertaken about what makes some communities and some nations happier than others. This research begins with the principle that happiness can be objectively measured. Being happy seems to contribute directly to good health. Secondly, being rich doesn't make anyone happy. You only have to look at all the millionaire sports stars to know that loads of cash and fame is the road to misery. They marry models, but still need to shag prostitutes; they take loads of drugs and booze and end up in rehab or prison; most are on at least their second marriage and their kids end up messed up and hating them. I have obviously over-generalised a bit, as there are some lovely celebrity folk out there with solid stable families.

"Work is vital, if that is what you want, but it is also important that the work is fulfilling. Perhaps the most important issue is the extent to which you have control over what you do. There is a creative spark in each of us, and if it finds no outlet, we feel half-dead. This can be literally true: among British Civil Servants of any given grade, those who do the most routine work experience the most rapid clogging of the arteries."
~ Richard Layard

It is also important, and a constant challenge, to get a balance between life, love and work. If you have a job you really enjoy, it is easy to want to do it more and more, at the expense of the rest of your life. If you have a very well paid job, your ego will convince you that the money and status are the things that are making you happy and you chase those things at the expense of your friends and loved ones. Balance is the key.

Many countries in the developing world with low income levels per capita are just as content as developed nations, and in some cases happier. Internationally, once people achieve an average income of about $15,000 per year, anything they earn above that level doesn't make them any happier.

Layard defines his 'Big 7' factors that affect happiness (listed in no particular order):

Family relationships: Countries with the highest rates of divorce and family break-up have relatively unhappy populations.

Financial situation: Not earning enough for your needs, or feeling pressurised to earn competitively for reasons of status, tends to lead to less happiness.

Work: Being under-employed or economically inactive makes us unhappy; doing relatively fulfilling work acts as a positive. "When people become unemployed, their happiness falls much less because of the loss of income than because of the loss of work itself."

Community and friends: Having active friendship groups and being involved in community activity and associations increases happiness.

Health: Poor health, particularly where it involves pain and distress, naturally leads to unhappiness.

Personal Freedom: Having some independence in our life decisions helps us to be happy.

Personal Values: Being of service to others, contributing to society and having a personal faith are all factors that may increase happiness.

I think this pretty much backs up what we have looked at so far.

Even in developed countries there appears to be maximum annual income for optimum happiness and contentment, which is about $75,000. In developed countries there are apparently two type of happiness: your day-to-day mood, (i.e. whether you feel stressed or content), and your 'life satisfaction.' The latter is a sort of smug, 'my life is going in the right direction' sort of happiness. According to the people who did the research for this (Daniel Kahneman and Angus Deaton) *'Higher incomes don't bring happiness, but they do bring you a life you* think *is better.'*

It's good to have a job and work, whether paid or voluntary, despite what your ego may be telling you. I understand that not all of us have a choice, especially during tough economic times, but I don't know anyone who has opted not to work who is really happy sitting at home drinking tea or down the pub all day, unless they are doing something on the side, which they are not declaring, like growing a marijuana plantation in their attic. A wise man once said to me, *"If you're ever tempted to jack your job in or retire early simply because you're bored, take some time off and watch daytime TV for a few days. You'll soon be dying to get back to work!"*

As soon as you are earning enough to take care of your basic needs, such as food, shelter, and safety, for you and your family, as well as some simple luxuries, like a holiday, you have the foundation for a happy life. Add a mix of friends, and social and community activities and, as long as you have your health, that's pretty much all you need. The Porsche, Rolex, fur coat and diet of caviar and champagne may be a fun distraction for a bit, but they will not add anything significant in the long run. You only have to look at the long list of celebrities who have died before their time to realise that all this stuff is not conducive to happiness. Elvis, Michael Jackson, Paula Yates, Karen Carpenter, Janis Joplin, Heath Ledger and Marilyn Monroe had it all, but still managed to self-destruct and die in their own individual tragic circumstances.

"Joy has nothing to do with material things or with a person's outward circumstance. A man living in the lap of luxury can be wretched, and a man in the depths of poverty can overflow with joy."
~ William Barclay

Stop Making Comparisons
The Fear of Missing Out, or FOMO

Keeping up with the Joneses is a thankless business. I am not sure how they do it, but they always have the latest stuff. Apparently, depressed people make more comparisons with others, and feel less worthy as a result. Happy people rarely compare, unless it is to learn something positive from someone they admire. I've heard that the Joneses are a miserable lot anyway, despite their big house, posh holidays and flashy cars.

Now I dare say that this sort of envy and fascination with other people's lives and possessions has been around since the dawn of time. Mr Caveman would have coveted Mrs. Cavewoman next door, and no doubt also had his eye on their new spear and carved bone handle club. With the advent of digital, social networking, it appears that it is all getting a bit out of hand, and has turned into an addiction known as FOMO – Fear of Missing Out. This is fundamentally the fear that everyone else is having a better time than you are.

64

In the old days, if you were happy and enjoying doing something simple, such as going for a walk, that was enough, but now it is so easy to see what other people are doing that it is tempting to spend more time watching other people's lives instead of actually living your own.

I have been at parties (very loud, drunken ones, I hasten to add) where friends of mine have been so busy posting pictures on Facebook to impress their friends who were at a different party, that they totally missed the best bits of the party they were actually at. Where is the sense in that?

FOMO can turn into a slavish desperation to make the most out of every social occasion. I have seen people accept invitations to several parties on the same evening. They have then used social media to make instant comparisons in order to determine which event they will ultimately attend. I personally think this is rude and selfish, and it rarely works out as planned. In hindsight, the other events were better and invariably you will not be invited again because you let someone down and made them feel second best.

Constantly comparing your life to others is a thankless task because you are only seeing the edited bits they want to share: the new car, the exotic trip to the Caribbean, the latest designer clothes. You are not seeing the credit card bill, the arguments with their partner because they take 3 hours to get ready, and the hangovers.

Rules and Boundaries

The free spirits and anarchists amongst you are not going to like this bit, but I think that we all need some clarity and direction, as well as work and love, in our lives. Kids are a great example of this. They don't think they like rules and boundaries, but they are always seeking them and pushing them to their limits. Happy kids generally have people around them who give them clear rules and boundaries. This guidance can vary massively depending on individual attitudes and culture, but if you scratch the surface, they are always there.

While we are looking at other clever people's ideas on life and happiness, it is worth considering Dr. Chérie Carter-Scott's rules of life from her book, *If Life is a Game, These are the Rules.* Dr. Chérie has a PhD in human and organisational development and 30 years' experience with this sort of thing. These are what she refers to as "universal truths"… meaning they are not really rules, but more like some unavoidable aspects of life:

Rule One: You will receive a body.
Whether you love it or hate it, it's yours for life, so accept it. What counts is what's inside that body of yours.

Rule Two: You will be presented with lessons.
Life is a constant learning experience, (heroic quests) which provides opportunities for you to learn more nearly every single day. These lessons are specific to you, and learning them is the key to discovering and fulfilling the meaning and relevance of your own life. Don't freak out when things don't go your way; everything happens for a reason. When I lost the house I wanted (as mentioned earlier), I was upset for ages but I ended up in a far nicer house in a better area for the same money!

Rule Three: There are no mistakes, only lessons.
Your development towards wisdom is a process of experimentation, trial and error, so it is inevitable things will not always go to plan or turn out how you'd want. Compassion is the remedy for harsh judgement of ourselves and others. Forgiveness is not only divine; it's also 'the act of erasing an

66

emotional debt'. Behaving ethically, with integrity and with humour, especially the ability to laugh at yourself and your own mishaps, are central to the perspective that 'mistakes' are simply lessons we must learn.

I failed some pretty important educational exams when I was younger because I did not work hard enough. I was bitterly disappointed and felt like I had let myself and my parents down. The easiest thing to do from then on would have been to avoid all exams and under-achieve for the rest of my life, but it's not in my nature to quit, so I vowed that if I was going to take an exam, I would commit to it properly and do my best. I'm still not brilliant at them but now when I get a poor result I know it is not due to a lack of hard work.

Rule Four: The lesson is repeated until learned.
Lessons are repeated until learned. Events that manifest as problems and challenges, irritations and frustrations are more lessons; they will repeat until you see them as such and learn from them. Your own awareness and your ability to change are requisites of executing this rule. According to Albert Einstein, the definition of Insanity is doing the same thing over and over again and expecting different results. Also fundamental is the acceptance that you are not a victim of fate or circumstance; 'causality' must be acknowledged. Things happen to you because of how you are and what you do. To blame anyone or anything else for your misfortunes is an escape and a denial; you yourself are responsible for you and what happens to you. Patience is required. Change doesn't happen overnight, so give it time to happen.

Rule Five: Learning does not end.
While you are alive there are always lessons to be learned. Surrender to the 'rhythm of life', don't struggle against it. Commit to the process of constant learning and change; be humble enough to always acknowledge your own weaknesses;

and be flexible enough to adapt from what you may be accustomed to, because rigidity will deny you the freedom of new possibilities.

Rule Six: There is no better than here.
The other side of the hill may be greener than your own, but being there is not the key to endless happiness. Be grateful for, and enjoy, what you have and where you are on your journey. Live in the present. Appreciate the abundance of what's good in your life, rather than measure and amass things that do not actually lead to happiness. Living in the present helps you attain peace.

Rule Seven: Others are only mirrors of you.
You love or hate something about another person according to what you love or hate about yourself. Be tolerant; accept others as they are and strive for clarity of self-awareness; strive to truly understand and have an objective perception of your own self, and your thoughts and feelings. Negative experiences are opportunities to heal the wounds that you carry. Support others, and by doing so you support yourself. Where you are unable to support others, it is a sign that you are not adequately attending to your own needs.

Rule Eight: What you make of your life is up to you.
You have all the tools and resources you need to be happy. What you do with them is up to you. Take responsibility for yourself. Learn to let go when you cannot change things. (Meditation can help with this.) Don't get angry about things; bitter memories clutter your mind. Courage resides in all of us, so use it when you need to do what's right for you. We all possess a strong natural power and adventurous spirit, which you should draw on to embrace what lies ahead.

Rule Nine: Your answers lie inside of you.
Trust your instincts and your innermost feelings, whether you hear them as a little voice or a flash of inspiration. Listen to feelings as well as sounds. Look, listen, and trust. Draw on your natural inspiration.

Rule Ten: You will forget all this at birth.
We are all born with all of these capabilities, but our early experiences lead us into a physical world, away from our spiritual selves, so that we become doubtful, cynical and lacking belief and confidence.

If you want to learn more about your inner voice and how you can train it to be more positive, try reading, *Learned Optimism-How to Change Your Mind and Your Life,* by Dr. Martin Seligman. This is an amazing, evidence based investigation into learning how developing an encouraging, optimistic attitude can significantly enhance quality of life for you and your fellow human beings.

With regard to Rule Ten, this is a very personal and spiritual subject; however, I have found a lot of answers in Eastern teachings and philosophies. One of the most acclaimed books in this field is *The Tibetan Book of Living and Dying* by the Buddhist master Sogyal Rinpoche. A very good friend of mine works for Rinpoche at a retreat in Ireland and says that he is incredibly humble, compassionate and inspiring. I have found his work fascinating and at times challenging, but ultimately vey illuminating.

These ten rules are not commandments; they are universal truths that apply to us all. When you lose your way, call upon them. Have faith in the strength of your spirit. Aspire to be wise because wisdom is the ultimate path of your life, and it knows no limits other than those that you impose on yourself.

I only read the rules of life recently, and thank goodness they echo what I have so far concluded myself, on my own. If I ever meet Dr. Chérie (and I hope I do), I will buy her a large drink. Then I will give her a huge life-affirming hug.

Ralph Waldo Emerson (1803-1901) is attributed to saying that "Life is a journey, not a destination" and he should know as he had a very long and eventful life. This can sometimes sound a bit patronising, especially if you feel a bit fed up with the journey, but there is actually a lot of truth to this, which we will investigate in the next chapter which considers the physical aspects of happiness and how your body can help you feel healthier and more contented.

5. The Joy of the Quest is in the Journey

Most of us know that regular exercise helps to keep us fit and healthy; the best way to lose weight is to eat less and move more. However, it is now also commonly recognised that exercise is an important element in maintaining mental health and achieving happiness.

Exercise releases endorphins in the brain, which in turn cause us to have what is commonly known as a 'natural high' or a 'runner's high'. You may not realise what caused it, but most of us have felt it at some time. During exercise, whether it is a long walk or a crazy downhill mountain bike ride, most people have experienced a moment when they suddenly forget about pain or discomfort, and are filled with a sense of euphoria. We have endorphins to thank for these moments of perfection.

Endorphins are chemicals produced in the brain, which bind to neuro-receptors to give relief from pain. Endorphins are also said to enhance the immune system, reduce stress and delay the aging process.

Exercise stimulates the release of endorphins, sending these chemicals throughout the body. Endorphin release varies from person to person. Some people will feel an endorphin rush, or second wind, after jogging for 10 minutes; others will jog for half an hour before their second wind kicks in.

Endorphin release can also result from meditation, acupuncture, massage, eating chillies, abdominal breathing and, of course, sex – I thought that would get your attention. Not just a load of old science stuff now is it? These activities all cause your body to produce endorphins naturally.

This is what Wikipedia has to say about these lovely little endorphins:

"Endorphins are endogenous opioid polypeptide compounds. They are produced by the pituitary gland and the hypothalamus in invertebrates during exercise, excitement, pain, consumption of spicy food, and orgasm, and they resemble the opiates in their abilities to produce analgesia and a feeling of well-being. Endorphins work as natural pain relievers."

Exercise also uses up excess adrenalin that we accumulate throughout the day due to situations that, as cavemen, we would have run away from or had a fight with. If we don't 'burn off' the excess adrenalin, we can suffer from stress. Your adrenal glands release large amounts of the stress hormones, adrenalin and cortisol, which shoot a burst of glucose and fatty acids into your blood for energy, increase your heart rate, breathing rate and blood pressure; blood rushes to your larger muscles, reducing the blood supply to your stomach, bowels, skin and extremities; your blood thickens (to stem any bleeding from injury) and your immune and digestive systems shut down (if you survive the lion, then you can eat and fight infection again).If you don't burn off this adrenalin, it will accumulate and result in stress.

If you are suffering from stress, I suggest you speak to your family doctor. You can also try reading more about it so that you understand what is happening to you physically and mentally. I found another book by Geoff Thompson particularly helpful, *A Book for The Seriously Stressed; How to Stop Stress from Killing You.*

Research suggests that regular physical activity appears as effective as psychotherapy for treating mild to moderate depression. Clinicians also report that patients who exercise regularly simply feel better and are less likely to overeat or abuse alcohol and drugs. [1]

Exercise can reduce anxiety, and people who exercise tend to feel less stressed or nervous. Even 5 minutes of aerobic exercise, such as jogging, swimming, cycling or walking, can stimulate anti-anxiety effects.

Most of us appreciate a drink now and then, but alcohol has an immediate effect on your mood, senses and physical co-ordination; the more you consume, the greater the effect. While these short-term effects may result in nothing more than a hangover, binge drinking and drinking too much can cause long-term effects on your health, specifically liver damage.

Similarly non-prescription drugs (and there are loads out there) can give you a short-term, 'quick fix' sense of euphoria and happiness, but these feelings are short-lived, and long-term use of drugs can, and probably will, affect your future health.

"A vigorous five mile walk will do more good for unhappy, but otherwise healthy, adults than all the medicine and psychology in the world."
~Dr. Paul Dudley White

Research on depression and exercise dates back almost 200 years. Many recent studies have reported the mood enhancing benefits of exercise in both healthy and clinically depressed

---

[1] *Just a quick note on drugs and booze. Alcohol may make you happy in the short term, but it can change the chemistry of your brain, increasing your risk of depression. If you already suffer from depression, drinking could affect your medication and put you at greater risk of anxiety.*

individuals. Most studies show depression and exercise to have psychological and physiological benefits for participants, with 90% reporting depression relieving effects.

The Mayo Foundation for Medical Education and Research suggests that exercise probably helps ease depression in a number of ways, which may include:

Releasing feel-good brain chemicals that may ease depression (neurotransmitters and endorphins)

Reducing immune system chemicals that can worsen depression.

Increasing body temperature, which may have calming effects.

Exercise has many psychological and emotional benefits too. It can help you:

Gain confidence. Meeting exercise goals or challenges, even small ones, can boost your self-confidence. Getting in shape can also make you feel better about your appearance.

Take your mind off worries. Exercise is a distraction that can get you away from the cycle of negative thoughts that feed anxiety and depression.

Get more social interaction. Exercise may give you the chance to meet or socialise with others. Just exchanging a friendly smile or greeting as you walk around your neighbourhood can help your mood.

Cope in a healthy way. Doing something positive to manage anxiety or depression is a healthy coping strategy. Trying to feel better by drinking alcohol, dwelling on how badly you feel, or hoping anxiety or depression will go away on their own can lead to worsening symptoms.

Now don't start thinking that you need to transform yourself into a spandex-clad fitness freak overnight to feel the benefits. To start with any extra exercise will help; build up slowly at a pace that suits you.

To get the maximum benefit from exercise, aim to do 30 minutes a day about five days a week, or 45 minutes to an hour at least three times a week. You don't have to do a solid half hour either. Find three ten-minute slots each day if that suits you, or two quarter hours.

Exercise can also boost your self-confidence and self-esteem. Dr. Alan Cohen, a GP with a special interest in mental health, says, "When people get depressed or anxious, they often feel that they're not in control of their lives. Any type of exercise is useful as long as it suits you and you do enough of it. Exercise should be something you enjoy; otherwise it will be hard to find the motivation to do it on a regular basis."

Okay, that's all well and good, I hear you say, but what is the best exercise to burn off excess adrenalin, improve my mood and make me feel healthy and in control? Well, that is entirely up to you, as different exercises suit different people. When I'm stressed and in need of letting off a bit of steam, I love a big cycle ride in the countryside or a 30 to 40 minute run. My wife prefers to go for long walks; my mum likes nothing better than a challenging yoga session; and my best friend likes to punch the hell out of a heavy bag. Whether it is an hour in the gym lifting weights or a cardio workout on a treadmill, the options are vast, and the best way to find your perfect exercise is to have a go and find out for yourself. If you're tired, exercise can give you energy; if you're worried, it can take your mind off your concerns for a while. Even a 15-minute walk can help you to clear your mind and relax.

I don't want to alienate anyone reading this who, for any reason, may not be able to carry out physical exercise. As discussed in Chapter 3, meditation is another way of achieving the mental health benefits described above, and if you combine both, then you really are on the right path to finding true and lasting happiness.

"Those who think they have not time for bodily exercise will sooner or later have to find time for illness."
~ Edward Stanley

It is now time to take the leap of faith and answer the call to adventure. You were probably not ready, too busy or just not listening hard enough to respond to it before, but now there is simply no avoiding it. You have come this far and I can see your inner hero peeking out from behind that bush, so let's set some goals and continue with the quest until we reach the prize.

6. The Call to Adventure

OK, I have laid out the case for happiness and tried to suggest what makes us unhappy, so let's try and fit this into a nutshell so it is a bit more useable:

The present is not a problem because you know that you can handle it. (See Chapter 1), I know it is in the past and just a memory now, but please do try and keep up, we are nearly there!

If anything happens that you don't like, it will become a past memory almost instantly and memories can be changed or forgotten with time.

Your expectations and ideas of success are positive and realistic. However, you are not going to let your happiness depend on them, so the future will be fine too.

Try living as happily as you can 'in the now' without trying to live up to the constant pressure of expectations of others, or dwelling on the past.

I saw on TV recently that there is a remote tribe (South America, I believe) where people are happy with simply getting on with day-to-day life, on a moment-to-moment basis. They apparently have no word for yesterday and no word for tomorrow.

Proper Planning and Preparation Prevents Poor Performance

First, make happiness your goal.

"Happiness is the No.1 goal of most people, and yet the majority have no idea of what would actually bring them this so-called happiness, or indeed have any sense of direction in life."
~ Dave Pelzer, 'A Child Called It.'

All workable, successful plans need to be **S.M.A.R.T**. This is a well-known, well-loved acronym representing, **S**-specific, **M**-measurable, **A**-achievable, **R**-realistic and **T**-Timetable.

Basically, your plan needs a very clear and **Specific** goal. For example, discover an inspiring quote every day. Next, it needs to be **Achievable**; in this case you are required to find a motivating quote each day and record it in a notebook or calendar. The task also needs to be Achievable and **Realistic**. Setting a goal of running a marathon with no training would be de-motivating and probably impossible for most people. Finding something inspiring every day may take some effort and research; however, it is achievable and realistic. And finally, you need a **Timetable**; in this case you may want to find one quote every day for a year. If you had not already guessed from reading the chapter titles, this is how I've completed the objective of writing this book!

Writing down your goals helps cement them in your mind and in your subconscious. Having the goals written down helps you make them happen. Once you've written them down, look at them at regular intervals. Evaluate your progress and decide if you need to revaluate them or change their focus or timeframe.

When you look at your goals periodically, you'll know where you stand and what you still need to accomplish.

A colleague of mine who used to be a competitive amateur body builder had the good fortune to meet Arnold Schwarzenegger during the 1980s. Not wanting to miss out on getting some free advice from the best body builder on the planet at the time, Simon asked Arnie how he had achieved so much coming from such humble beginnings. This is Simon's interpretation of Arnie's advice that night, and it basically involves four simple but powerful steps to achieving goals.

1. Know exactly what you want and visualise what it looks like.
2. Make alliances with people who can help you on your quest.
3. Focus on, and accentuate, the positives.
4. Eliminate or neutralise the negatives.

Whatever you think of Mr. Schwarzenegger, there is no denying that he knows how to achieve a goal when he sets his mind to it, so this seems to be pretty solid, effective advice.

There is a famous story about a Harvard Business School study conducted on students in an MBA program. In that year, students were asked, "Have you set clear, written goals for your future and made plans to accomplish them?" Only 3% of the graduates had written goals and plans, 13% had goals, but they were not in writing; 84% had no specific goals at all. The story goes that, ten years later, the members of the class were interviewed again with the following findings: the 13% of the class who had goals were earning, on average, twice as much as the 84% who had no goals at all. What's more, the other 3% who had clear written goals were earning, on average, ten times as much as the other 97% put together. Now I am not suggesting you focus on earning loads of money, I am just using this as an example of how effective a tool writing your goals down can be.

It can be very powerful to write a philosophy specific to your own needs that you can use to focus your mind on what is important to you and what makes you happy.

This is an example of what I have used to remind myself, as simply as possible, of the things that resonate with me and have helped me. This is by no means the finished 'philosophy' because as long as I am alive, I will be experiencing and learning, but at this time this is how I try to focus my mind on my own quest for happiness:

I will be happy now and I will make the effort to be happy every day.

I would rather be happy than rich. Optimism is the key to happiness.

I will deal with life's challenges one day at a time.

I will relax with life and flow with it.

Prioritisation

Making decisions can be very stressful for many people. As we have already established, there are just so many choices and options out there. With this in mind, there is a simple tool that can help you prioritise what you need to do so that you make decisions based on good practice to get the important stuff out of the way quickly. Leaving things to the last minute is stressful, and often means that you miss out jobs that really need to get done.

The first task you need to do when prioritising is to write a list of tasks that need doing. I know loads of people who write lists and work through them indiscriminately. This can lead to some major stress, especially if you are planning a wedding and buying the rings ends up at the bottom of your list whilst buying beer for your stag party is at the top.

Prioritisation is the key. It takes a bit of effort and skill, but once you get the hang of it, it is incredibly liberating and powerful. The most relaxed and successful people I know are really good at prioritising, and it shows because they always appear calm, organised and prepared.

Put very simply, you can split the things you need to do into four categories:

DO, DELEGATE, DEFER or DUMP (See Figure 2):

Figure 2. The 'Urgent and Important' priority matrix

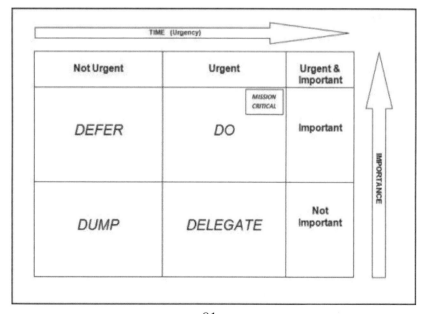

DO – If something is really important and needs to be done urgently, it takes priority over everything else and gets done first. For example, if you get a red electricity bill that says you will be cut off at 12 o'clock today, you need to get it sorted very quickly or you won't be able to watch your favourite TV programme later and the freezer will defrost. Of course, there can be something more urgent that crops up, such as if you break your leg. This then becomes the highest priority (sometimes known as mission critical), and even overrides the electricity bill, because it is dangerous to your health and hurts like hell!

DELEGATE – If something is not so important, but needs to be done urgently, you can ask someone else to do it. I can see you control freaks stressing out over this already. Delegation is a skill that can free up your time so that you can get on with the really important things in your life that you genuinely can't let anyone else do. If I am working from home and someone in my house is going out, I often ask them to post letters for me or pick up the dry cleaning, so that I can carry on with the work I need to finish that has a deadline.

Delegation can be extremely useful because an interruption during the performance of a task distracts you for 3-4 times the length of the interruption. It takes your brain that long to get back into the flow. A 5 minute interruption can take up to 15 minutes before you are back in the zone. This is why it is also very important to 'protect' your time when you have a very important task to complete by switching off your phone or even hanging a 'do not disturb' sign on your door.

DEFER – If a task is important, but there is no urgent deadline, you can defer it and carry on with a DO or a DELEGATE task instead. This can be something like mowing the lawn. Nobody is going to die if you don't mow the lawn, but it will become urgent when you can't find the cat, so it will eventually move up the priority list.

DUMP – If something on your list of things to do is not important and there is no deadline, it can get dumped in preference to DO, DELEGATE or DEFER. You can do these tasks when you eventually have the luxury of spare time. Just make sure that if you do DUMP a job it won't mess things up for someone else.

Below is an example of a un- prioritised and prioritised list of things to do, determined by using the Do, Delegate, Defer, Dump principle.

Un- prioritised List.

1. Buy toothpaste.
2. Mow the lawn.
3. Pay the electricity bill.
4. Prepare dinner.
5. Book your train ticket for next week.
6. Wash the car.
7. Book hotel for business trip next week.
8. Help daughter with homework.
9. Post letter.
10. Clean out garage.
11. Visit your friend in hospital.

Prioritised List

1. Pay the electricity bill. – **Do it now!**
   Urgent & Important: If it is not paid by today we will be cut off!
2. Visit your friend in hospital. – Do!

Urgent & Important. Only you can do this and he needs your support today.

3. Help daughter with homework. – Do.
   Important but not as Urgent, but it does need to be in by tomorrow.

4. Prepare dinner. – Delegate.
   Urgent but not Important. You need to eat but it's only a salad, so ask the kids to help.

5. Buy toothpaste. – Delegate.
   Urgent but not Important. Ask partner to get some on the way home from work.

6. Book hotel for business trip next week. – Delegate.
   Urgent but not Important. Ask appropriate person at work to help.

7. Book your train ticket for next week. – **Defer.**
   Important but not Urgent. You need to do it yourself but it's not urgent.

8. Mow the lawn. – **Defer.**
   Important but not Urgent. It's not urgent but it does need doing before it gets too long.

9. Post letter. – **Defer.**
   Important but not Urgent. It's not urgent so you can do it next time you pass a post box.

10. Clean out garage. – **Dump.**
    Not Urgent & not Important. You haven't done it for years anyway.

One last tip before we leave prioritisation and move on to change: There is a Spanish phrase that, roughly translated, means *"Start the day by eating the live frog!"* It basically means that you should start your day by getting the worst and most unappetising task out of the way as soon as possible. If you don't, you will spend most of your day worrying about it while you could be getting on with being happy.

So there we are, you need never be stressed or miss a deadline again. Happy days.

Change

"If you don't like something, change it. If you can't change it, change your attitude."
~ Maya Angelou

I realised several years ago that the job I once loved had changed... and it had taken over my life. My work-life balance was extremely one-sided in favour of work, and I was not spending enough quality time with my family and friends. The two most important people in my life, my wife and baby daughter, were getting the tired grumpy end of the bargain, and I realised that this was not good for them or good for me. The problem was that something needed to change, and the only person who could change it was me. The options were to let change happen to me – I could have a nervous breakdown, get a divorce and start a new life – or I could revaluate my goals and proactively make changes that would simplify my life so that I could be genuinely happy and a benefit to my family.

I decided to change my job and downscale the responsibility and perceived importance of my career. My ego did not like this and insisted that I would lose respect from my peers and would be unable to have as much fun if I took a pay cut and reduced my status and power in a new company. My old friend 'doubt' literally stopped me in my tracks for a while. I remained a slave to my salary. Then I remembered to write down what I wanted to achieve and, specify how I was going to change and what would make me happy. I wanted more time and less stress and responsibility whilst maintaining a comfortable standard of living.

One of the major problems was that my job involved driving over 35,000 miles a year, which was dangerous, time consuming and stressful in itself. Most of these miles were done before and after work hours driving to and from appointments. Simply by cutting down my miles, I could reduce stress and gain more time. I now drive about 20,000 miles a year, which does not sound like a big decrease, but I reckon I have gained at least an extra 200 hours (25 working days) a year when I am not stuck in a metal box on a dangerous motorway to nowhere. Result!

When you go through major change, the emotions you experience are similar those of bereavement. You therefore go through the process outlined in the Elisabeth Kübler-Ross model, commonly known as **The Five Stages of Grief**: Denial, Anger, Bargaining, Depression and Acceptance. As part of my job, I had been trained in change management, so I was expecting to go through a rollercoaster of emotions. This is pretty much what happened to me, so it was reassuring to know what was happening and why. It helped me stay with the commitment I had made to change and understand the feelings I was going through at any one time.

I did not realise at first, but as soon as I subconsciously knew it was time for change I was already at the first step of the five cycles:

DENIAL: *"It's not the job it's me, it's bound to change soon".*

This was quite short-lived and quickly turned to **ANGER:** *"Everyone I work with is an idiot. If everyone would just do their bloody job properly, I wouldn't have to sort everything out all the time."*

Then came the **BARGAINING:** *"OK, I'll stay another month and ask for more money, then we will take an exotic holiday and it will all be fine."*

Eventually, the **DEPRESSION** hit, and I did feel as if there was no hope; that I would either be stuck in a rut forever and potentially lose my family or I would burn out and fade away. New jobs were not forthcoming and I was rejected by one company that I was banking on to get me out of my situation.

This period was the toughest and seemed to last for ages even though it was only a few months. I read the inspiring quotes I had written in my special quote book (more quotes from my special book later) and one actually worked. It helped focus my mind and pull me out of the tail spin I was in:

"Success is how high you bounce when you hit the bottom."
~ General Patton

With **ACCEPTANCE**, the 5th and final stage, came a huge sense of relief. I knew that my old job was no longer right for me and that change was essential. Everything happens for a reason, and I was not meant to get the job at the company that rejected me; obviously it was not right for me or for them. I would have to start again with a new company, building new relationships and forging trust. It was going to be demanding and uncomfortable, but it had to be done as the alternatives were not healthy for me or my family. The challenge now was to enjoy the change and use all the tricks and tips I had learned to make the journey as enjoyable and comfortable as possible, which it has been, even though it has required regular and concerted effort. The result is that I have more time to dedicate to my family and maintaining my happiness; it has also given me the opportunity to write this book.

Just a quick note regarding depression; if you are really feeling depressed, it is essential that you talk to someone. A problem shared really is a problem lessoned. Depression also may require professional help. If you are concerned, you really should get specialised medical advice as soon as you can from your doctor or a suitable healthcare professional.

Back to the Future! Visualisation and Optimism

As we considered right at the start of all this, our future exists in our expectations. If you are facing change or contemplating your future, it is worth preparing for it properly; in other words, not leaving anything to chance. Visualisation is a very powerful tool. **Imagine** what is going to make you happy, **feel** it, and then **do** it. If you visualise empty, unrealistic stuff that your ego tells you will make you happy, then you are setting yourself up for a fall; so consider what we have looked at and make your imaginations authentic and good for your soul. Remember to keep it simple and reasonable, and don't attach too much importance to it. If it works out, brilliant; if it does not, that is fine, too. Remain optimistic and have another go.

I try to visualise myself and my family being happy, healthy and financially secure enough not to have to worry too much about money. I am a relentless optimist (to the annoyance of some people!) and always try to the upside of a situation.

Apparently your brain cannot tell the difference between a real and an imagined action. According to Lynne McTaggart in her book, *The Intention Experiment,* electromyography (EMG) has shown that the brain does not differentiate between the *thought* of an action and a *real* action. In an experiment with a group of skiers, EMG revealed that, when they mentally rehearsed their downhill runs, the electrical impulses sent to the muscles were the same as when they were physically engaged in the runs. It appears that, just as when they were really performing an activity, imagining that the activity stimulated certain neural pathways and produced chemicals, so it was that the same physiological changes were present. Whether the activity is carried out in reality or is imagined, it appears that the neural pathways are strengthened.

This is a technique used by the Austrian ski legend, Herman Maier. The "Herminator" ranks as one of the finest alpine ski racers in history. He won four overall World Cup titles, two Olympic Gold medals, three World Championship titles and 54 races on the World Cup circuit. If you watch footage of him before a race, he stands at the start gate at the top of the run with his eyes closed. He is visualising the whole run in real time from take-off to winning finish, twitching, crouching and grimacing as if he is really doing it: no fear, no mistakes; just flat-out perfection.

When I was considering changing my job, my ego and my general fear of change filled me with doubt and dread. As we have established, this is natural and is mostly due to adrenalin. In order to fight back, I imagined the type of work life balance I would like and how I was going to get it. This helped me find the right job for me. Then I prepared for interviews by visualising myself as being totally organized, optimistic (instead of scared), confident and in control. I visualised the interview going well and being offered the job, and how I would accept it and look forward to my new career. I truly believed I was right for the role and this obviously came through in the interview. I know it did, in fact, because over a drink one night I actually asked the interviewer how it all went and the feedback was very positive; exactly as I had planned and visualised it.

Learning from your mistakes is also a key aspect of visualisation. I have to come clean here and admit that I had two interviews before the successful one, and they did not go so well. However, I took the feedback and visualised doing things better the next time with the desired result.

"If you always do what you've always done you'll always get what you've always got."
~ Henry Ford

Many years ago, the University of Chicago conducted a famous study with basketball players to prove the power of visualisation. It involved three basketball teams, each of whom were given different instructions:

Team 1 was instructed to go to the gym every day for 1 hour and practice throwing free throws.

Team 2 spent an hour in the gym every day, followed by a visualization period in which they envisaged themselves successfully shooting hoops. No physical practice was allowed.

Team 3 was instructed to play no basketball whatsoever, neither mentally or physically for the month.

When the month had passed, the three groups were assessed to determine if their shooting had been affected. The team who had neither mental nor physical practice had not improved, and had in fact got a bit worse. The team who engaged in just physical practice had a 24% improvement rate. Amazingly, the team who had only visualized themselves throwing successful free throws had improved by 23%.

There you go... what about that then! All you gamers and couch potato athletes would be pretty amazed at what you could accomplish if you visualized it first and then actually tried it for real!

Visualisation Tips and Techniques

Visualisation is creating a mental picture of something. It is powerful because it makes the future clearer. Seeing yourself already achieving your goal makes your brain believe that attaining that goal is possible, exactly as described in the basketball study.

(1) When visualising, it's essential to view the action in the first person, i.e. see yourself achieve your goal through your own eyes, rather than watching yourself from the outside. This method is most effective because this is the way you really see and experience everything already.

(2) If you are having difficulty visualising something, relax and try studying a picture or photo closely; then close your eyes and try to remember what you see. If you see anything like the picture, you are visualising.

(3) Make visualisation as real as possible; the more real your image is, the better it works. Try to imagine smells, colours, textures, sounds, emotions, tastes... everything you can imagine to make it as vivid as possible. Make it real time and full of movement, not just a static picture.

(4) Relax: don't stress about how well you're seeing, feeling, hearing, etc. Relaxation is a necessary part of the visualisation process. The more you try to force it, the more you will fail to see positive results.

Have a go and enjoy the experience. It should be fun, and if it isn't, try visualising something else that is.

Now that you are in the right frame of mind, it is time to cross the threshold and take the next step on the quest. Once you have experienced even the briefest taste of living in the now, I promise you will never look back.

7. Crossing the Threshold and Accepting the Quest

It is generally accepted by psychologists that it takes about 28 days to create a new habit or break an old one. This means that you must invest in your future happiness by making the effort to live optimistically for 4 weeks, consciously focusing on the things that you have established that make you genuinely happy.

After 28 days, one of two things can happen: you will either revert back to your former habits, or you will keep this change. If you do revert back to old habits, then you have lost nothing and hopefully you will have benefited both physically and mentally from a month of optimistic thinking. Generally, smokers take three or four real concerted goes at giving up smoking before they quit for good, so don't beat yourself up if you do go back to your old ways; simply revisit the things that worked for you and have another go at it. Happiness takes effort, and even the most enlightened and contented masters practise and refocus every day.

Like anything worth achieving, you need to make an effort to be happy, and this takes planning and preparation.

First thing's first: **Start the day** with the intention to be happy and do everything in your power to help this intention along.

1) Smile and tell yourself to be optimistic and that you want to enjoy today. It takes 17 muscles to smile and 42 to frown. Use motivational thoughts or quotes. Write them down where you can see them frequently if that helps. Saying them out loud is even more effective.

2) Have breakfast – when you are hungry or your blood sugar is low it is not uncommon to feel a bit slow and vulnerable,

so get some food in you as soon as possible. It is called breakfast because you need to break the fast your body has been subject to where you were asleep.

3) Listen to a piece of music that inspires you or makes you feel good. Sing along. Close your eyes (if you're not driving, of course) and enjoy the feelings that the song/music evokes.

4) "Start the day by eating the live frog! *(see the prioritisation bit in Chapter 6)*

5) Read something that will do the same (more on this later).

6) If you have a partner or family, make the effort to tell them you love them and give them a kiss before you all go your separate ways for the day.

7) Do some stretching or yoga, go for a walk, run or swim, do anything that makes you feel alive and gets your blood moving.

8) Plan to do something nice for someone else even if it is just making them a cup of tea.

9) If it winter time and you are feeling a bit low because of the lack of sunshine, remember how you felt on a summer's day by thinking about a special holiday or looking at some holiday photos that make you happy. It is no uncommon to suffer from SAD (Seasonally Affected Disorder) or the 'winter blues' to some degree. If this is true for you, it might be worth investing in a UV light box or simply trying to get outside as much as possible during the winter months. Try to get a desk by a window or even get up an hour earlier to get an extra hour's worth of daylight.

Before you go to sleep count your blessings... and write them down

Last thing before going to bed, write down three things that went well today and made you feel good. Writing things down more is more effective and powerful than just thinking about them, or at the very least, say them out loud.

Intentions for the next day.

Start each say by getting the worst job out of the way first (back to eating the frog again as discussed in the prioritisation section of Chapter 5.)

One factor that ensures people act on their intentions is 'implementation intentions' or 'situational cues'. These provide concrete, external stimuli that jog the memory. For example, if you want to go for a run tomorrow morning, facilitate that intention by putting your trainers by the bed; "The moment I get up, I'm going to put on those trainers and go out for my run." Some people procrastinate because they only have vague intentions. If you have a general intention, you need to make it much more specific. In order to follow up your intentions, provide yourself with cues to remind you of what you are supposed to be doing.

I believe that happiness is a choice, and simple act of reading this book suggests that you want to choose happiness. Well done, by the way.

"Until one is committed, there is hesitancy, the chance to draw back, always ineffectiveness. Concerning all acts of initiative and creation, there is one elementary truth, the ignorance of which kills countless ideas and splendid plans: that the moment one definitely commits oneself, then providence moves too.

95

All sorts of things occur to help one that would never otherwise have occurred. A whole stream of events issue from the decision, raising in one's favour all manner of unforeseen incidents, meetings and material assistance, which no person could have dreamed would have come their way. Whatever you can do or dream you can, begin it. Boldness has genius, power and magic in it. Begin it now. "
~ Johann Wolfgang Von Goethe

Commit to trying to *be* happy instead of deciding *when* you are going to be happy. The fact that you have chosen to read this far means that you are already a few steps down the path, so why not carry on? You've done the hardest bit, which is recognising and starting the whole process.

Don't be scared if it works; you should enjoy being happy and be able to share it with someone else. So what are you waiting for? Oh yes, I forgot, you will start when you have more time, when the kids grow up, or when you move house, etc., etc. I know I sound like I'm nagging, but we all need to be nudged a bit at the start. You obviously want a bit of a kick in the pants or you would have stopped reading this by now, so I am not going to apologise for being a bit pushy.

"May every sunset bring you peace and every sunrise bring you hope. "
~ Unknown

8. The Art of Living Heroically

Whether making a formal presentation or verbally explaining an idea, the golden rule is "Tell them what you going to tell them, tell them and then tell them what you told them", and we have now arrived at the "tell them what you told them" bit.

We started this quest looking at past, present and future. Now we are going to pull it all together as a guide for the journey to living like the hero that you are. Living heroically is an art, and like all skills it takes focus and practice.

Today is the Most Important Day of Your Life

You can't change the past, but you can ruin the present by worrying about the future!

The past is gone, so remember the good bits and let go of the bad, because there is nothing you can do to change what has already happened. The future exits in our expectations, so make your expectations realistic and don't let your happiness depend on whether you achieve them or not. "Focus on what you have and your life will be full; focus on what you do not have and your life will be empty."

Say to yourself, "Whatever happens, I will be able to handle it." The present is the tiny fleeting gap between the past and the future, so try to live in the present and appreciate the beauty and simplicity that surrounds you every day. As we established in Chapter 1, "There are no perfect people or perfect lives, only perfect moments." Trust yourself, and face the present with the right attitude and you'll find happiness.

So... the present is not a problem because you know that you can handle it. If anything does happen that you don't like, it will become a memory almost instantly and memories can be modified or forgotten with time.

Your expectations are positive and realistic, and you are not going to let your happiness depend on them, so the future will be fine too!

Try living as happily as you can "in the now", without trying to live up to the constant pressure of the expectations of others or dwelling on the past.

Even the Bravest Hero Feels Fear

Don't mistake the natural feelings associated with adrenalin for fear; they are completely natural and everybody feels them. The antidote to adrenalin is single minded optimism and action. Positive thinking is extremely powerful.

Adrenalin + Optimism + Action = Courage & Strength

Adrenalin + Pessimism + Inaction = Fear & Weakness

It's better to be an optimist who is sometimes wrong than a pessimist who is always right.

Challenges and Tests are Unavoidable

Life is a mystery that the human mind is not capable of comprehending; some mysteries are simply not supposed to be understood.

Trust that everything is happening perfectly as part of a grand design; pain and suffering is unavoidable and optimism is the antidote.

Life may have no real purpose other than to become a better person day by day. It is an opportunity to discover what makes you happy and what your gifts or talents might be, and to learn how to be at peace and content with who you are.

Whether you like it or not, life is a never ending series of heroic quests, and you are the hero, with an ability to handle the tests and trials, and appreciate the perfect moments.

Let Go and Release Your Inner Hero

Let go of the past and dump the baggage. Unhappiness is due to preoccupation with oneself. "Knowing oneself" is critical to self-development, but you should remember not to become fixated with you! Worrying is praying for what you don't want! Forgiveness is healing. Revenge is toxic. And meditation is a gift.

"My actions are my only true belongings. I cannot escape the consequences of my actions. My actions are the ground upon which I stand."
~ Nhat Hanh

"Love and work, work and love ... that's all there is."
~ Sigmund Freud

The Joy of the Quest is in the Journey

Exercise is an important element in maintaining mental health and achieving happiness. It releases endorphins in the brain, which in turn cause us to have a "natural high". Exercise, as well as keeping you physically fit to face the challenges of the world, burns off excess adrenalin, which helps to reduce anxiety and protects your body against stress. Do more exercise!

Crossing the Threshold and Accepting the Quest

Understand what you want and make happiness your goal. *"Happiness is the No.1 goal of most people and yet the majority have no idea of what would actually bring them this so-called happiness, or indeed have any sense of direction in life."*
~ Dave Pelzer

Prioritisation saves you time and stress and makes life a lot more straightforward and easy to manage.

Change is a process that requires focus and commitment.

"If you don't like something change it. If you can't change it, change your attitude."
~ Maya Angelou

Art of Living like a Hero

Happiness takes commitment, and even the most enlightened masters practise and refocus every day. Like anything worth

100

achieving you need to make an effort to be happy. This takes planning and preparation. It is generally accepted by psychologists that it takes about 28 days to create a new habit or break an old one, so make the decision to change now.

We have now come to the final and possibly the most important element of the Heroic Quest philosophy.

Happiness Requires Daily Effort

Now you know the secret to achieving lasting happiness you simply need to focus your efforts and not forget the hard and well-earned lessons you have learned in your life so far.

Today is the first day of the rest of your life. It is now time to head out on your quest and face life's tests and trials, with the support of friends that you will meet along the way. Your ultimate goal is to develop ability deal with life one challenge at a time. Appreciate the moments of perfection, and adopt an optimistic attitude in order to cope with the tough times in between. Step by step, moment by moment; living in the now! It is a challenge but the rewards are infinite.

Know the path; walk the path! It is one thing to know the path, but it takes dedication and effort to actually get up off your butt and walk it. I nicked this from a good friend of mine who is an excellent motivator, coach and trainer. His name is Phil and he's an Aikido master, so I thought I had better give him a mention simply out of respect.

The basic gist of this bit of wisdom is that it is all well and good reading the books and knowing the theories, but it is absolutely pointless unless you use them and put them into practice, every day.

To be truly happy requires practise, effort and discipline, in order to fight the daily battle with your ego.

I have trawled the universe and ancient scriptures for pearls of wisdom to help you with your daily battle against the mental chatter that your ego will continually throw at you, in order take you off the straight and narrow, and lead you toward a life in the pursuit of things that you don't really need and that could even make you miserable. Hidden amongst these pearls of wisdom is the actual answer to the secret of your true happiness. Really, I'm not joking; this is powerful stuff.

You can read them over and over again, because through the wonders of memory, they will probably mean something completely different to you each time you read them.

"There is always a first step in a thousand mile walk."
~ Confucius *(and you appear to have taken it, so well done again.)*

"No matter how far you have gone on the wrong road, it's never too late to turn back."
~ Proverb *(I blame sat nav for this one.)*

You know what to do, and how to do it, but everyone needs a boost now and again, so here are 365 of the wisest friends and helpers who have ever walked the earth, to help you achieve your goals and return with the prize.

Celebrate your success and remember to smile loads, smiling releases endorphins and makes you feel better. It also makes people wonder what you have been up to!

9. Friends and Helpers to Support you on Your Quest

I guarantee that if you adopt a heroic attitude, and face life one step at a time, you will become stronger and happier every day. Tough times don't last but tough people do.

Practise the three elements of the Heroic Quest philosophy every day and remember that you are the hero of your own life story, so start living heroically now.

The Heroic Quest Philosophy:

Today is the most important day of your life.

Challenges & tests are unavoidable.

Happiness requires daily effort.

January

1. Let go of yesterday and stop worrying about tomorrow, so you don't end up ruining today.
   ~ *Unknown*

2. Don't judge a person by their appearance, a possession by its value, a day by the weather or health by any degree of pain.
   ~ *Marlo Morgan, 'Message from Forever'*

3. In daily life we must see that it is not happiness that makes us grateful, but gratefulness that makes us happy.
   ~ *Brother David Steindl-Rast*

4. Fear is where we go to learn.
   ~ *Unknown*

5. It is only possible to live happily ever after on a day to day basis.
   ~ *Margaret Bonnano*

6. We are what we repeatedly do; excellence then is not an act but a habit.
   ~ *Aristotle*

7. Worrying is praying for what you don't want.
   ~ *Sharon Gannon*

8. If you're going through hell, keep on walking.
   ~ *Winston Churchill*

9. We cannot direct the wind, but we can adjust the sails.
   ~ *Unknown*

10. Worry does not empty tomorrow of troubles, it empties today of its strength.
    ~ Unknown

11. You can't get yourself out of a hole until you recognise that you are in one.
    ~ Unknown

12. I try to avoid looking forward or backward, and try to keep looking upward.
    ~ Charlotte Bronte

13. Everyone smiles in the same language.
    ~ Unknown

14. Today is the tomorrow I worried about yesterday and all is well.
    ~ Unknown, taken from a fridge magnet

15. If you observe a really happy man you will find him building a boat, writing a symphony, educating his daughter, growing roses in his garden. He will not be searching for happiness as if it were a collar button that has rolled under the radiator.
    ~ W. Beran Wolfe

16. No winter lasts forever; no spring skips its turn.
    ~ Hal Borland

17. When life knocks you down, try to land on your back. Because if you can look up, you can get up.
    ~ Les Brown

18. People who say it cannot be done should not interrupt those who are doing it.
    ~ Chinese proverb

19. Too much thinking never made anyone happy.
   ~ *Unknown*

20. Always look at what you have left. Never look at what you
   have lost.
   ~ *Robert H Shuller*

21. Success is getting what you want. Happiness is wanting what
   you get.
   ~ *Dale Carnegie*

22. If you see ten troubles coming down the road, you can be
   sure that nine will run into the ditch before they reach you.
   ~ *Calvin Coolidge*

23. Real security is based on wanting less not having more.
   ~ *Unknown*

24. Miracles happen to those who believe in them.
   ~ *Bernard Berenson*

25. Fear is a shadow; information is the light.
   ~ *Unknown*

26. Law of abundance – be prepared to give and you will
   receive; the most powerful gifts cost nothing at all.
   ~ *Unknown*

27. As we grow older we discover we have two hands. One for
   helping ourselves and one for helping others.
   ~ *Audrey Hepburn*

28. You will never be happier than you expect. To change your
   happiness, change your expectation.
   ~ *Bette Davis*

29. When I hear somebody sigh, "life is hard", I am always tempted to ask, "Compared to what?"
~ *Sydney J. Harris*

30. I cannot escape the consequences of my actions. My actions are the ground upon which I stand. My actions are my only true belongings.
~ *Thich Nhat Hanh*

31. Don't judge each day by the harvest you reap, but by the seeds you plant.
~ *Robert Louis Stevenson*

February

1. Take risks; if you win you'll be happy and if you lose you'll be wise.
   ~ *Unknown*

2. I have become my own version of an optimist. If I can't make it through one door, I'll go through another door or I'll make a door.
   ~ *Rabindranath Toagore*

3. Happiness is as a butterfly which, when pursued, is always beyond our grasp, but which if you will sit down quietly may alight upon you.
   ~ *Nathaniel Hawthorne*

4. Trust yourself; you know far more than you think you do.
   ~ *Benjamin Spock*

5. We must accept finite disappointment, but we must never lose infinite hope.
   ~ *Martin Luther King Jr.*

6. The world is so fast that there are days when the person who says it can't be done is interrupted by the person doing it.
   ~ *Unknown*

7. People spend a lifetime searching for happiness; looking for peace. They chase idle dreams, addictions, religions, even other people, hoping to fill the emptiness that plagues them. The irony is the only place they ever needed to search was within.
   ~ *Ramona L Anderson*

8. Keep smiling – it makes people wonder what you've been up to.
   ~ *Max Eastman*

9. We've got to convince our egos and our minds that, if we want to live happy lives, love is more important than anything else!
   ~ *Ken Keyes*

10. Sometimes your joy is the source of your smile, but sometimes your smile can be the source of your joy.
    ~ *Thich Nhat Hanh*

11. Love is the master key that opens the gates of happiness.
    ~ *Oliver Wendell Holmes*

12. Most misunderstandings are due to poor communication.
    ~ *Unknown*

13. What soap is to the body, laughter is to the soul.
    ~ *Yiddish proverb*

14. When you harbour bitterness, happiness will dock elsewhere.
    ~ *Andy Rooney*

15. I hear and I forget, I see and I remember, I do and I understand.
    ~ *Confucius*

16. Opportunities are never lost; someone will always take the ones you miss.
    ~ *Unknown*

17. There is a wonderful mythical law of nature that the three things we crave most in life - happiness, freedom, and peace of mind – are always attained by giving them to someone else.
    ~ Peyton Conway March

18. Hope for the best, but prepare for the worst.
    ~ Proverb

19. When walking through the valley of shadows, remember, a shadow is cast by a light.
    ~ H. K. Barclay

20. Happiness is not so much in having as sharing. We make a living by what we get, but we make a life by what we give.
    ~ Norman MacEwan

21. People who have drawn wealth into their lives used The Secret, whether consciously or unconsciously. They think thoughts of abundance and wealth, and they do not allow any contradictory thoughts to take root in their minds.
    ~ Rhonda Byrne

22. Since you get more joy out of giving joy to others, you should put a good deal of thought into the happiness that you are able to give.
    ~ Eleanor Roosevelt

23. Change takes guts, imagination and commitment.
    ~ John Taylor

24. Anything's possible if you've got enough nerve.
    ~ J. K. Rowling

25. By engaging our fears we dispel them. If they are poison, we immunise ourselves by swallowing small, regular doses.

Once our fears become familiar, they lose their hold over us.
~ *Unknown*

26. Feeling gratitude and not expressing it is like wrapping a gift and not giving it.
    ~ William Arthur Ward

27. When ignorance is mutual confidence is king.
    ~ *Chinese proverb*

28. Simply put, you believe that things or people make you unhappy, but this is not accurate. You make yourself unhappy.
    ~ *Wayne Dyer*

29. **Extra one for leap years**: It is not work that kills men; it is worry. Work is healthy; you can hardly put more upon a man than he can bear. Worry is rust upon the blade. It is not the revolution that destroys the machinery, but the friction. Fear secretes acids, but love and trust *are sweet juices.*
    ~ *Henry Ward*

March

1. When you plan to get even with someone you are only letting that person continue to hurt you.
~ *Carleen Roxas*

2. An optimist is a person who sees a green light everywhere, while the pessimist sees only the red stoplight. The truly wise person is colour blind.
~ *Albert Schweitzer*

3. Learn to be calm and you will always be happy.
~ *Paramhansa Yogananda*

4. To be happy you either need the ability to forgive or a poor memory.
~ *Unknown*

5. Life is what happens when you're busy making plans.
~ *John Lennnon*

6. Success is not the key to happiness. Happiness is the key to success. If you love what you are doing, you will be successful.
~ *Albert Schweitzer*

7. A pessimist is one who makes difficulties of his opportunities; an optimist is one who makes opportunities of his difficulties.
~ *Harry Truman*

8. Happiness is nothing more than good health and a bad memory. The grand essentials of happiness are: something to do, something to love and something to hope for.
~ *Albert Schweitzer*

9. Two things you should NEVER say to the one you love: "I love you, but..." and "If you loved me, you would..."
   ~ *Unknown*

10. We all live with the objective of being happy; our lives are all different and yet the same.
    ~ *Anne Frank*

11. Happiness cannot be travelled to, owned, earned, worn or consumed.
    ~ *Denis Waitley*

12. Smile - it increases your face value.
    ~ *Unknown*

13. Happiness is the spiritual experience of living every minute with love, grace and gratitude.
    ~ *Denis Waitley*

14. You can never get enough of what you don't need to make you happy.
    ~ *Eric Hoffer*

15. Pessimism never won any battle.
    ~ *Dwight David Eisenhower*

16. Action may not always bring happiness, but there is no happiness without action.
    ~ *Benjamin Disraeli*

17. Gratefulness is the key to a happy life that we hold in our hands, because if we are not grateful, then no matter how much we have we will not be happy, because we will always want to have something else or something more.
    ~ *Brother David Steindl-Rast*

18. Life can be tough, but you can be tougher.
    ~ Unknown

19. Few things in the world are more powerful than a positive push. A smile. A word of optimism and hope. A "you can do it" when things are tough.
    ~ Richard M. DeVos

20. A man isn't poor if he can still laugh.
    ~ Raymond Hitchcock

21. A smile is a powerful weapon; you can even break ice with it.
    ~ Unknown

22. There are at least two days a week that you should not worry about, yesterday and tomorrow.
    ~ Unknown

23. Happiness is when what you think, what you say, and what you do are in harmony.
    ~ Mahatma Ghandi

24. Avoid the need to use force by projecting strength.
    ~ Japanese proverb

25. If you want **others** to be happy, practice compassion. If **you** want to be happy, practice compassion.
    ~ 14th Dalai Lama

26. In the middle of difficulty lies opportunity.
    ~ Albert Einstein

27. What we call the secret of happiness is no more a secret than our willingness to choose life.
    ~ *Leo Buscalglia*

28. Let us be grateful to people who make us happy; they are the charming gardeners who make *our souls blossom.*
    ~ *Marcel Proust*

29. That man is the richest whose pleasures are the cheapest.
    ~ *Henry David Thoreau*

30. It's only money; you can get more of it!
    ~ *Mark Nubold*

31. For myself I am an optimist, it does not seem to be much use being anything else.
    ~ *Winston Churchill*

April

1. Success is how high you bounce back when you hit the bottom.
   ~ General George S. Patton

2. Life does not care about your plans.
   ~ Buddhist proverb

3. There came a time when the risk to remain tight in the bud was more painful than the risk it took to blossom.
   ~ Anais Nin

4. The tortoise only makes progress when he sticks his neck out, however his ass is always covered.
   ~ Unknown

5. Life is full of misery, loneliness, and suffering - and it's all over much too soon.
   ~ Woody Allen

6. One's mind once stretched by new ideas never regains its original dimensions.
   ~ Oliver Wendell Holmes

7. A friendly look, a kindly smile, one good act, and lives worthwhile.
   ~ Unknown

8. There is only a thin line between the sublime and the ridiculous.
   ~ Unknown

9. The noisiest person in the room is often the weakest.
   ~ Unknown

10. To laugh often and love much... to appreciate beauty, to find the best in others, to give one's self... this is to have succeeded.
    ~ *Ralph Waldo Emerson*

11. If something is too good to be true then it probably is.
    ~ *Old adage*

12. Whatever is to make us better and happy, God has placed either openly before us or close to us.
    ~ *Lucius Annaeus Seneca*

13. With change comes opportunity.
    ~ *Unknown*

14. Discovery consists of seeing what everybody has seen and thinking what nobody has thought.
    ~ *Albert Szent-Gyorgyi*

15. In the land of the blind the one-eyed man is king
    ~ *Desiderius Erasmus*

16. The minute you start to talk about what you're going to do if you lose, you have lost.
    ~ *Unknown*

17. Turn a setback into comeback.
    ~ *Unknown*

18. The most difficult part of getting to the top of anything is getting through the crowd at the bottom.
    ~ *Unknown*

19. It is a sign of strength, not of weakness, to admit that you don't know all the answers.
    ~ *John P. Loughrane*

20. We always believe our first love is our last, and our last love our first.
~ *Unknown*

21. Once we accept our limits, we go beyond them.
~ *Albert Einstein*

22. FEAR – Fantasy Expressed As Reality.
~ *General wisdom*

23. Optimism is the foundation of courage.
~ *Nicholas Murray Butler*

24. You always miss 100% of the shots you do not take.
~ *Wayne Gretzky*

25. Little deeds of kindness, little words of love, help to make earth happy like the heaven above.
~ *Julia F. Carney*

26. No one can make you feel inferior without your permission.
~ *Eleanor Roosevelt*

27. Only dead fish swim with the tide.
~ *Unknown*

28. The brave may not live forever, but the cautious may not live at all.
~ *Ambrose Redmoon*

29. Cheaters never win and winners never cheat.
~ *Unknown*

30. You never saw a very busy person who was unhappy.
~ *Dorothy Di*

May

1. It's never too late to start.
   ~ Unknown

2. The best way to cheer yourself up is to try to cheer somebody else up.
   ~ Mark Twain

3. When you find yourself in a hole, stop digging!
   ~ Will Rogers

4. Think big thoughts, but relish small pleasures.
   ~ H. Jackson Brown, Jr.

5. Never say no to a gift from a child.
   ~ Unknown

6. Caring is the ultimate competitive advantage.
   ~ Unknown

7. Most people would rather be certain they're miserable than risk being happy.
   ~ Robert Newton Anthony

8. Don't slam the door shut forever; you may want to go back in one day.
   ~ Don Herald

9. Investigate before you speculate.
   ~ Good practice

10. Nobody really cares if you're miserable, so you might as well be happy.
    ~ Cynthia Nelms

11. Don't throw away the old bucket until you know if the new one holds water.
    ~ *Swedish proverb*

12. Stare up the steps then step up the stairs.
    ~ *Unknown*

13. Happiness makes up in height for what it lacks in length.
    ~ *Robert Frost*

14. The way to really get things done is to not mind who gets the credit for doing them.
    ~ *Benjamin Jowett*

15. The world's most successful people are rarely the most talented; they are the most confident.
    ~ *Unknown*

16. There is always one moment in childhood where the door opens and lets the future in.
    ~ *Graham Greene*

17. Unhappiness is due to preoccupation with oneself.
    ~ *Unknown*

18. Do something. Lead, follow or get out of the way.
    ~ *Thomas Paine*

19. Happiness isn't something you experience; it's something you remember.
    ~ *Oscar Levant*

20. To follow by faith alone is to follow blindly.
    ~ *Benjamin Franklin*

21. Put your future in good hands; your own.
    ~ *Unknown*

22. For things to change we must change. For things to get better we must get better.
    ~ *Unknown*

23. How we spend our days is of course how we spend our lives.
    ~ *Annie Dillard*

24. One of the best ways to persuade others is with your ears, by listening to them.
    ~ *Dean Rusk*

25. Happiness is a choice that requires effort at times.
    ~ *Aeschylus*

26. Listen to your dreams – those are the sounds no one else can hear.
    ~ *Kobi Yamada*

27. It gets dark sometimes, but morning comes and with it, the light.
    ~ *Jessie Jackson*

28. The night is darkest just before the dawn.
    ~ *Thomas Fuller*

29. Doing what you love is the cornerstone of having abundance in your life.
    ~ *Wayne Dyer*

30. Dreams don't die until we let them.
    ~ *Unknown*

31. In daily life we must try to see that it's not happiness that makes us grateful but gratefulness that makes us happy.
~ *Unknown*

June

1. The bravest sight in the world is someone fighting against the odds.
   ~ Franklin K. Lane

2. The tragedy of life is not that it ends too soon, but that we wait so long to begin it.
   ~ W. M. Lewis

3. If you don't start out the day with a smile, it's not too late to start practicing for tomorrow.
   ~ Unknown

4. Every moment in your life, including this one, is a fresh start.
   ~ B. J. Marshall

5. Nobody who ever gave his best regretted it.
   ~ George Halas

6. A happy man is too satisfied with the present to dwell too much on the future.
   ~ Albert Einstein

7. Great things are achieved by a series of small things being brought together.
   ~ Vincent Van Gogh

8. Change is not merely necessary in life; it is life.
   ~ Alvin Toffler

9. Be happy while you're living, for you're a long time dead.
   ~ Scottish proverb

10. What you can't get out of, go into wholeheartedly.
   ~ *Mignon McLaughlin*

11. To find an open road you need an open mind.
   ~ *Welsh proverb*

12. You can do anything, but you can't do everything.
   ~ *Unknown*

13. Not all birds fly. What separates the flyers form the walkers is the desire to take off.
   ~ *Nepalese proverb*

14. Just do your best every day.
   ~ *Sian Groom - advice to her daughter*

15. Learn from your mistakes and your successes.
   ~ *Unknown*

16. If you see something broken, fix it.
   ~ *Common sense*

17. When you generate momentum, keep it going.
   ~ *Unknown*

18. Celebrate your successes or you won't have any more.
   ~ *Unknown*

19. Regret of wasted time is more wasted time.
   ~ *Mason Cooley*

20. It's not the size of the dog in the fight; it's the size of the fight in the dog.
   ~ *Mark Twain*

21. Don't let the perceptions of others change your behaviour; let your behaviour change the perceptions of others.
   ~ Unknown

22. Choose to face the challenges of each day with despair or serenity.
   ~ Eastern philosophy

23. Discomfort is where the action is. All the gold is neatly stacked in great abundance behind the wall of fear that most of us dare not even attempt to surmount.
   ~ Unknown

24. A smile confuses an approaching frown.
   ~ Unknown

25. Remember whom you work for; your family.
   ~ Unknown

26. Happiness is the ability to dwell on the good things in life and not the bad.
   ~ Unknown

27. Evil prospers when the good do nothing.
   ~ Edmunde Burke

28. Wisdom is not the acquisition of knowledge; it's knowing which knowledge is worth acquiring.
   ~ Unknown

29. Be thankful for the problems you face at work. If things were less difficult, someone with less ability would have your job.
   ~ Unknown

30. Ability is what you are capable of; motivation determines what you do and attitude determines how well you do it.
~ *Lou Holtz*

July

1. If you want to earn more you've got to learn more.
   ~ *Unknown*

2. Do not ASSUME as it can make an ASS of U and ME.
   ~ *Lots of people*

3. We do not own our children; they only pass through us
   on their way to the world.
   ~ *Unknown*

4. Want what you've got.
   ~ *Sian Groom*

5. A gift has real value when it hurts a little to give it.
   ~ *Buddhist teachings*

6. If you don't like something, change it. If you can't
   change it, change your attitude to it.
   ~ *Maya Angelou*

7. Pain is temporary – quitting lasts forever.
   ~ *Lance Armstrong*

8. Progress is achieved by looking around, not just looking
   ahead.
   ~ *Unknown*

9. If you want happiness, cherish others not yourself.
   ~ *Sogyal Rinpoche*

10. A smile is an inexpensive way to improve your looks.
    ~ *Unknown*

11. Feel the fear and do it anyway.
    ~ *Susan Jeffers*

12. Good friends are hard to find, difficult to keep and
    impossible to forget.
    ~ *Unknown*

13. A friend is someone who understands your past, believes
    in your future, and accepts you just the way you are.
    ~ *Unknown*

14. Luck is years of preparation meeting a moment of
    opportunity.
    ~ *Oprah Winfrey*

15. Happiness doesn't come from doing what we like to do
    but from liking what we have to do.
    ~ *Wilfred A. Peterson*

16. Always remember to be happy because you never know
    who's falling in love with your smile.
    ~ *Unknown*

17. Any intelligent fool can make things bigger, more
    complex and more violent. It takes a touch of genius and
    a lot of courage to move in the opposite direction.
    ~ *Albert Einstein*

18. Happiness is in your own serenity.
    ~ *Tibetan Buddhist teaching*

19. Do not have anything in your home that you do not deem
    to be useful or believe to be beautiful.
    ~ *William Morris*

20. Destiny is a mysterious thing, sometimes enfolding a miracle in a leaky basket of catastrophe.
    ~ *Francisco Goldman*

21. Unhappiness is the over consideration of what others think of you.
    ~ *Unknown*

22. You don't stop playing because you get old, you get old because you stop playing.
    ~ *George Bernard Shaw*

23. Most people ask for happiness on condition. Happiness can only be felt if you don't set any condition.
    ~ *Margaret Lee Runbeck*

24. No matter where you go, there you are.
    ~ *Mad Max 2- The Road Warrior*

25. Before you put on a frown, make absolutely sure there are no smiles available.
    ~ *Jim Beggs*

26. Don't be afraid of the space between your dreams and reality.
    ~ *Ralph Waldo Emerson*

27. A person will be called to account on Judgement Day for every permissible thing he might have enjoyed but did not.
    ~ *Talmud*

28. The secret of contentment is knowing how to enjoy what you have, and to be able to lose all desire for things beyond your reach.
    ~ *Lyn Yutang*

29. The good life is a happy life. I do not mean that if you are good you will be happy; I mean that if you are happy you will be good.
   ~ Unknown

30. Success is getting what you want; happiness is wanting what you get.
   ~ Dale Carnegie

31. Adapt / Adopt / Improve.
   ~ Unknown

August

1. The purpose of life is the expansion of happiness.
   ~ *Maharishi Mahesh Yogi*

2. People are just as happy as they make up their minds to be.
   ~ *Abraham Lincoln*

3. There are plenty of obstacles in life, don't let yourself become one of them.
   ~ *Unknown*

4. Physical capabilities may be limited, but there are no laws that govern the will.
   ~ *Eddy Merckx*

5. Eighty percent of success is showing up.
   ~ *Woody Allen*

6. We don't see things as they are; we see things as we are.
   ~ *Anais Nin*

7. The trouble with the world is that the stupid are cocksure and the intelligent are full of doubt.
   ~ *Bertrand Russell*

8. Love of money is the root of all evil.
   ~ *Ancient Greek proverb*

9. KISS – Keep it simple, sweetheart.
   ~ *Unknown*

10. Misery loves company.
    ~ *Proverb*

11. Don't pray for an easy life; pray to be a strong person.
    ~ Unknown

12. The only thing worse than a bad decision is no decision.
    ~ *Unknown*

13. Treat every day as if it's your last because one day you
    will be right!
    ~ *Unknown*

14. Living with fear is a lot scarier than confronting it.
    ~ *Unknown*

15. The feeling of fear (adrenalin) is as natural as the
    feelings of hunger and thirst. When you feel hungry you
    don't panic, you eat. When you feel thirsty you don't
    panic, you drink. So if it is fear, you don't panic, you do.
    ~ *Cus Damatio*

16. It takes less effort and fewer muscles to smile than it
    does to frown.
    ~ *Unknown*

17. Worry gives small things a big shadow.
    ~ *Swedish proverb*

18. It's easy to be brave from a safe distance.
    ~ *Aesop*

19. Fortes fortuna adviuvat (fortune favours the brave).
    ~ *Latin proverb*

20. Carpe diem (seize the day).
    ~ *Latin proverb*

21. Worry is a form of fear.
    ~ *Bertrand Russell*

22. Love grows by giving. The love we give away is the only love we keep. The only way to retain love is to give it away.
    ~ *Elbert Hubbard*

23. Lose the clouds and gain the sky.
    ~ *Tibetan Buddhist teachings*

24. Motivation requires a goal.
    ~ *Unknown*

25. Listening is an attitude of the heart, a genuine desire to be with another, which both attracts and heals.
    ~ *J. Isham*

26. It won't last forever; nothing does.
    ~ *Elizabeth Gilbert*

27. A calm mind welcomes wisdom.
    ~ *Tibetan Buddhist teachings*

28. In a nation of millions and a world of billions, the individual is still the first agent of change.
    ~ *Lyndon B. Johnson*

29. Treasure this day and yourself. Neither will ever happen again.
    ~ *Ray Bradbury*

30. Life is like sculpture; a matter of seeing what others can't then chiselling away the rest.
    ~ *Unknown*

31. A closed mouth gathers no foot.
   ~ Unknown

September

1. The best portion of a good man's life is his little, nameless, unremembered acts of kindness and love.
   ~ *William Wordsworth*

2. Standing your ground is progress if you are fighting a hurricane.
   ~ *Unknown*

3. Obstacles don't stop people, people stop people.
   ~ *Unknown*

4. When you are going around in circles, head for the middle.
   ~ *Mat Padwick*

5. Money – the more you have, the more you need, and the less you have, the less you miss it when it's gone.
   ~ *Unknown*

6. Real serenity is based on wanting less not having more.
   ~ *Eastern philosophy*

7. You cannot truly listen to anyone and do anything else at the same time.
   ~ *M. Scott Peck*

8. Fear less, hope more; Whine less, breathe more; Talk less, say more; Hate less, love more; And all good things are yours.
   ~ *Swedish proverb*

9. You can sometimes learn more from losing than you can from winning.
   ~ *Unknown*

10. Add life to your days not days to your life.
    ~ *Unknown*

11. The greatest weakness of most humans is their hesitancy to tell others how much they love them while they're still alive.
    ~ *O.A. Battista*

12. Ability is what you arc capable of; motivation is what you do; attitude determines how well you do it.
    ~ *Lou Holtz*

13. Be strong and supple like bamboo in order to ride out the storm.
    ~ *Japanese proverb*

14. A job begun is a job half done.
    ~ *Proverb*

15. In this world, the optimists have it, not because they are always right, but because they are positive. Even when they are wrong they are positive, and that is the way of achievement, correction, improvement and success. Educated, open-eyed optimism pays.
    ~ *David Landes*

16. It's better to be an optimist who is sometimes wrong than a pessimist who is always right.
    ~ *Unknown*

17. Start your day with the worst job.
    ~ *Phil Howman*

18. Life's a box of chocolates, Forrest. You never know what you're gonna get.
    ~ *Mrs. Forrest Gump*

19. Change is the only thing in life you can rely on.
    ~ *Buddhist teaching*

20. Create the world you dream with every choice you make.
    ~ *Stephen C. Paul*

21. If it was easy, everybody would do it.
    ~ *Unknown*

22. Always plan ahead. It was not raining when Noah built the ark.
    ~ *Richard C. Cushing*

23. Make stepping stones out of the stumbling blocks.
    ~ *Unknown*

24. Instead of seeing the rug being pulled from under us, we can learn to dance on a shifting carpet.
    ~ *Susan Jeffers*

25. Sod's Law – Nothing is as easy as it looks. Everything takes longer than you expect. If anything can go wrong it will, at the worst possible moment.
    ~ *Sod!*

26. In the long run the pessimist may be proved right, but the optimist has a better time on the trip.
    ~ *Daniel L. Reardon*

27. The foundation of understanding is the willingness to listen.
    ~ *Unknown*

28. Some people never say the words "I love you."
    It's not their style to be so bold.
    Some people never say those words "I love you."
    But, like a child, they're longing to be told.
    ~ *Paul Simon*

29. You have 2 ears and 1 mouth; use them in that proportion.
    ~ *Unknown*

30. One of the things I learned the hard way was that it doesn't pay to get discouraged. Keeping busy and making optimism a way of life can restore your faith in yourself.
    ~ *Lucille Ball*

October

1. Buy cheap, pay twice.
   ~ Unknown

2. You are the average of the five people you spend the most time with, including yourself.
   ~ John Rhot

3. Where fear is present wisdom cannot be.
   ~ Lactantius

4. Optimism is the one quality more associated with success and happiness than any other.
   ~ Robert Louis Stevenson

5. There are few monsters that warrant the fear we have of them.
   ~ Andre Gide

6. Obstacles are those frightful things you see when you take your eyes off your goal.
   ~ Henry Ford

7. Don't be afraid to go out on a limb; that is where the fruit is.
   ~ H. Jackson Browne

8. If you get knocked down seven times you must get up eight.
   ~ Unknown

9. Take the knocks and keep moving forward.
   ~ Unknown

10. Enter every activity without giving mental recognition to the possibility of defeat. Concentrate on your strengths instead of your weaknesses, on your powers instead of your problems.
~ *Paul J. Meyer*

11. Eat the world or it will eat you.
~ *Jewish proverb*

12. When you feel inspired, act.
~ *Unknown*

13. Think Strong; Feel Strong; Be Strong.
~ *Phil Groom*

14. Let your heart guide you. It whispers, so listen carefully.
~ *The Land Before Time - movie*

15. What does not kill me only makes me stronger
~ *Friedrich Nietzsche*

16. One day at a time, one hour at a time, one second at a time.
~ *Phil Groom*

17. There is no such thing as bad weather, only bad clothes.
~ *Proverb*

18. Security is not having things, it's handling them.
~ *Geoff Thompson*

19. Necessity may be the mother of invention, but play is certainly the father.
~ *Roger von Oech*

20. Stop the fight, start the flow, choose to be fearless, relax and let go.
~ *Phil Groom*

21. Stop listening to the mental chatter. Reduce the noise and ignore the negative.
~ *Unknown*

22. God give me the serenity to accept the things I cannot change, the courage to change the things I can, and the wisdom to know the difference.
~ *Reinhold Niebuhr*

23. Pushing through fear is less stressful than living with the underlying anxiety that comes from trying to control the world.
~ *Susan Jeffers, 'Five truths about fear'*

24. Say YES to the things we can't control.
~ *Unknown*

25. It is impossible for you to be angry and laugh at the same time. Anger and laughter are mutually exclusive, and you have the power to choose either.
~ *Wayne Dyer*

26. Life does not cease to be funny when people die any more than it ceases to be serious when people laugh.
~ *George Bernard Shaw*

27. He who binds himself to a joy, does the winged life destroy; He who kisses the joy as it flies, lives in eternity's sunrise.
~ *William Blake*

28. If you can control your thoughts, you can control your life.
    ~ *Rigpa teachings*

29. Humour helps us to think out of the box. The average child laughs about 400 times per day, the average adult laughs only 15 times per day. What happened to the other 385 laughs?
    ~ *Unknown*

30. We become anxious when bored. Relax and accept your fears.
    ~ *Unknown*

31. We are what we think and we think too much.
    ~ *Unknown*

November

1. Toleration is the greatest gift of the mind; it requires that same effort of the brain that it takes to balance oneself on a bicycle.
   ~ Helen Keller

2. React less; act more.
   ~ Unknown

3. If I were given the opportunity to present a gift to the next generation, it would be the ability for each individual to learn to laugh at himself.
   ~ Charles M. Schulz

4. If it happens, it happens, and if it does, I'll deal with it.
   ~ Geoff Thompson

5. Never lose a chance to say a kind word.
   ~ William Makepeace Thackeray

6. Try not to create too much hope or fear, for they only engender mental gossip.
   ~ Sogyal Rinpoche

7. Don't fear the dark or you will be afraid for half of your life.
   ~ Unknown

8. The two best physicians of them all - Dr Laughter and Dr Sleep.
   ~ Gregory Dean Jr.

9. The power of NO leaves you powerless; the power of YES makes you fearless.
   ~ Unknown

10. Don't paralyse yourself with anxiety today as you try to control the present and predict the future.
    ~ Unknown

11. Trust that you will survive whatever happens.
    Unknown

12. Better to regret the things you have done rather than the things you have not.
    ~ Unknown

13. Why be miserable when you can choose to be happy?
    ~ Unknown

14. You can discover more about a person in an hour of play than in a year of conversation.
    ~ Plato

15. Pain is weakness leaving the body.
    ~ US Marine Corps

16. Find something you love to do and you'll never have to work a day in your life.
    ~ Harvey Mackay

17. Cleverness is not wisdom.
    ~ Euripides

18. Use your imagination, not to scare yourself to death, but to inspire yourself to life.
    ~ Adele Brookman

19. Simplicity is the ultimate sophistication.
    ~ *Leonardo Da Vinci*

20. Continuity gives us roots; change gives us branches,
    letting us stretch and grow and reach new heights.
    ~ *Pauline R. Kezer*

21. Ships are safe in the harbour, but that's not what ships
    are for.
    ~ *William Shedd*

22. Fear is the friend of exceptional people. Make fear your
    friend.
    ~ *Geoff Thompson.*

23. If it was not SCARY everyone would do it.
    ~ *Unknown*

24. They may forget what you said, but they will never
    forget how you made them feel.
    ~ *Carl W. Buechner*

25. The dog that chases two rabbits catches neither.
    ~ *Proverb*

26. If you pray for rain you have to be prepared to deal with
    the mud.
    ~ *Denzel Washington*

27. Regardless of the severity of a setback, no matter how
    dreadful a blow you sustained, you can always find a
    bright side if you search hard enough. The key to
    happiness, success and mental health is to utterly ignore
    the negative, deny its power over you and find reason to
    celebrate every development in life including the
    cruellest catastrophe, by discovering the bright side to

even the darkest hour.

~ Dean Coontz, 'From the corner of his eyes'

28. Everybody has choice. Even the man in front of a firing squad can choose to fall to his knees and cry or pull down his blindfold and sing.

    ~ Proverb

29. Treasure the love you receive above all. It will survive long after your good health has vanished.

    ~ Og Mandino

30. Insanity is doing the same thing over and over and expecting a different result.

    ~ Albert Einstein

December

1. Choose life!
   ~ Unknown, seen on a t-shirt

2. The man who can push himself further when the pain kicks in will win.
   ~ Roger Bannister

3. The only things we can really control are our reactions to whatever life hands us.
   ~ Buddhist teachings

4. To fear love is to fear life, and those who fear life are already three parts dead.
   ~ Bertrand Russell

5. Strength does not come from winning. Your struggles develop your strengths. When you go through hardships and decide not to surrender, that is strength.
   ~ Arnold Schwarzenegger

6. If you want to do something, you find a way. If you don't want to do something, you find an excuse.
   ~ Unknown

7. Until you make peace with who you are, you will never be content with what you have.
   ~ Doris Mortman

8. Those who bring sunshine to the lives of others cannot keep it from themselves.
   ~ Sir James M. Barrie

9. Forgiveness means letting go of the past.
   ~ *Gerald Jampolsky*

10. You don't get to choose how you're going to die or when. You can only decide how you're going to live now.
    ~ *Joan Baez*

11. A misty morning does not signify a cloudy day.
    ~ *Proverb*

12. It's not who is right, but what is right that is of importance.
    ~ *Thomas Huxley*

13. We are all functioning at a small fraction of our capacity to live fully in its total meaning of loving, caring, creating and adventuring. Consequently, the actualizing of our potential can become the most exciting adventure of our lifetime.
    ~ *Herbert A. Otto*

14. Sunshine is delicious, rain is refreshing, wind braces us up, and snow is exhilarating; there is really no such thing as bad weather, only different kinds of good weather.
    ~ *John Ruskin*

15. There is no substitute for paying attention.
    ~ *Diane Sawyer*

16. It has been estimated that the average person has sixty thousand separate thoughts each and every day. The problem with this is that we have the same sixty thousand thoughts today that we had yesterday, and we'll repeat them again tomorrow.
    ~ *Wayne Dyer*

17. Happiness is not a state to arrive at but a manner of travelling.
    ~ Margaret Lee Runback

18. The life and love we create is the life and love we live.
    ~ Leo Buscaglia

19. We cannot become what we want to be by remaining who we are.
    ~ Ghandi

20. People don't fear the unknown, they fear losing the known.
    ~ Unknown (I'm not joking)

21. Some pursue happiness, others create it.
    ~ Unknown

22. You will find as you look back upon your life that the moments when you have really lived are the moments when you have done things in a spirit of love.
    ~ Henry Drummond

23. The only thing sadder than work unfinished is work never begun.
    ~ Christina G. Rossetti

24. The men who try to do something and fail are infinitely better than those who try to do nothing and succeed.
    ~ Lloyd Jones

25. Like gravity, karma is so basic we often don't even notice it.
    ~ Sakyong Mipham

26. Our deeds determine us as much as we determine our deeds.
    ~ *George Eliot*

27. Replace judgement with curiosity.
    ~ *Unknown*

28. Real power is the ability to do good things for others.
    ~ *Buddhist teachings*

29. The nature of rain is constant, but it can grow flowers in the meadow or thorns in the marsh.
    ~ *Proverb*

30. How people treat you is their karma; how you react is yours.
    ~ Wayne Dyer

31. We are what we repeatedly do.
    ~ *Aristotle*

The Heroic Quest Philosophy:

Today is the most important day of your life.
Challenges & tests are unavoidable.
Happiness requires daily effort.

6887809R00090

Printed in Great Britain
by Amazon.co.uk, Ltd.,
Marston Gate.